TRUTH,
JUSTICE,
AND POWER

The Jesus Way

TRUTH, JUSTICE, AND POWER

The Jesus Way

ADULT STUDENT BOOK

Compiled and Edited by Cheryl L. Price, Ph.D.

Urban Ministries, Inc.

Urban Ministries, Inc.

UMI (Urban Ministries, Inc.)
P. O. Box 436987
Chicago, Illinois 60643-6987
1-800-860-8642
www.urbanministries.com

First Edition

First Printing

Truth, Justice, and Power—The Jesus Way Student Book has been compiled and edited by Cheryl L. Price, Ph.D.

Library of Congress Cataloguing in Publications Data

ISBN-10: 1-63038-204-3

ISBN-13: 978-1-63038-204-9

Printed in the United States of America.

Cover Design and Layout by Aysling Creative Services

DEDICATION

This book is dedicated to all who seek and desire to know and share God's Word.

TABLE OF CONTENTS

DEDICATION. V

INTRODUCTION. IX

*CHAPTER 1 | GOD HAS A PLAN FOR US 1

Genesis 39:1–6, 16–23

CHAPTER 2 | MAKING A BOLD MOVE 9

Numbers 27:1–11

*CHAPTER 3 | INTERCESSORY PRAYER MEETING 18

2 Kings 19:14–21, 25–36

*CHAPTER 4 | GOD'S JUSTICE AND THE BURNING BUSH 27

Exodus 3:1–10

CHAPTER 5 | SEEKING SALVATION AND CHOOSING COMPASSION 37

Luke 10:25–37

CHAPTER 6 | WORSHIP ANCHORS MY SOUL. 48

John 4:7–24

*CHAPTER 7 | SHARE THE GOOD NEWS. 57

Mark 5:1–19

CHAPTER 8 | PRAISING GOD WITH A NEW STEP .64

Acts 3:1–10

*CHAPTER 9 | PROTECTION: WHO'S GOT YOUR BACK? 72

1 Samuel 19:1–7

CHAPTER 10 | WORK ETHIC: ADVANCING THE GOOD NEWS. 80

Acts 18:1–4, 18–26

*Recommended for five-day Bible curriculum

INTRODUCTION

In Ephesians 6:10–18, the Apostle Paul admonishes Christians to put on the "whole armor of God." Why would Paul tell believers to suit up with the protective covering of a soldier? Our answer lies in Paul's analysis of each piece of Christian "armor" we must wear as protective gear for battle against spiritual forces!

Paul begins with the belt of truth. Truth is the foundation upon which pieces of the armor are connected. He then discusses the breastplate of righteousness. Christ gives us the righteousness that strengthens our hearts to stand against Satan's attacks. Next, Paul addresses the covering needed for our feet so that the Gospel message can be shared with others. Paul also speaks about the shield of faith, used to defeat the flaming darts of the evil and wicked ways of Satan. Additionally, the helmet of salvation and the sword of Spirit represent the Word of God. Both the helmet and the sword afford the knowledge and understanding of God's Word believers need as they study. Paul concludes that the armor should be coated with the protection of prayer.

Although Paul uses imagery tied to the garb of Roman soldiers, we can apply the armor today like superheroes prepared to defend and fight for truth, justice, and power through Jesus. Poverty, racism, sexism, domestic violence, false advertisements, fake "reality" television shows, gossip, political circuses, computer hacking, bullying, and dropping out of school are some of the troubles and failures that plague our society.

Christians, like superheroes or soldiers, must fight and stand against these problems that have at their root spiritual forces and principalities. Often we struggle and want to defend our faith, but are not properly equipped. We waste our energy creating strategies, but wind up hitting the wrong targets.

As you read *Truth, Justice, and Power—The Jesus Way*, prepare to be challenged and strengthened to stand for truth, justice, and power. Participate in discovering or enhancing your biblical knowledge through group or individual studies. Use the Student Workbook (study guide) and actively share in Group Discussions, answering questions from the Observation and Interpretation of the Scriptural lesson, and decide to engage in the Personal and Community Application from the Student Book. A Leader's Guide is available to assist teachers in creating and implementing the lessons.

A snapshot of the 10 chapters of *Truth, Justice, and Power—The Jesus Way*:

Chapter 1 - God Has a Plan for Us—Overcoming Roadblocks to God's Purpose for Us
Chapter 2 - Making a Bold Move—Stand Up for Justice When Others Won't
Chapter 3 - Intercessory Prayer Meeting—There is Power in Prayer
Chapter 4 - God's Justice and the Burning Bush—God's Unusual Invitation to Moses
Chapter 5 - Seeking Salvation and Choosing Compassion—Choosing God Over Religious Traditions
Chapter 6 - Worship Anchors My Soul—Worship is a Matter of the Heart
Chapter 7 - Share the Good News—Unashamed to Share the Good News of Christ
Chapter 8 - Praising God with a New Step—Healing on the Way into Prayer Service
Chapter 9 - Protection: Who's Got Your Back?—Standing for Justice and Truth against the Opposition
Chapter 10 - Advancing the Good News—Teaching Teachers Who Teach God's Word

Be a soldier, a superhero prepared and ready to stand for *Truth, Justice, and Power—The Jesus Way*!

CHAPTER 1

GOD HAS A PLAN FOR US

SCRIPTURE LESSON

Genesis 39:1–6, 16–23

BACKGROUND SCRIPTURES

Genesis 21:22, 26, 37:1–36; Psalm 1:3, 8:6, 105; Proverbs 6:23–24

QUESTION

Often it is extremely hard to see, much less understand, that God has a plan for us. In light of the many things that can and do go wrong every day, how do we keep moving while realizing that God has not forgotten us? Certainly, the loss of hope and the feeling of being alone make real our thought that we have been forgotten by the One who made us. In an effort to move beyond these feelings, how do we reassemble and refocus our faith, so that we keep moving, and embrace the fact that our lives are in God's hands, that He loves and knows what's best for us?

GOD HAS A PURPOSE FOR OUR LIVES

Fredrick Morris is the great-great-grandson of Frederick Douglass. Morris tells the story of Douglass' learning how to read despite many obstacles. Initially, his master's wife taught him the alphabet; she intended to do more until her husband made her stop and ensured Douglass would not have the opportunity to pick up a book, let alone learn how to read. However, Frederick Douglass befriended some White boys and convinced them to teach him how to read. This was the first of many steps for Frederick Douglass that shaped him into a prominent American abolitionist who fought against injustice for both African Americans and women. He changed the political and social landscape for African Americans, and became their voice and hope. Douglass demonstrates the sum total of what God can do with someone who started out with nothing. God can do great things for a person who keeps moving despite obstacles.

DISCUSSION

Certainly, many of us will never know the struggle of wanting to read but lacking the opportunity or resources. However, if we wanted to learn and those in power hoarded the resources and limited our opportunities, how many of us would stand up and demand (as our ancestors did) access to books, teachers, and other resources to achieve? With our family social structure and (for some) the value of education in decline, how many would fight for access to greater knowledge? How many of us will trust God for strength to live the life He desires for us despite present and future obstacles? How many of us will trust the plan God has for our lives?

TRANSITION

Our lesson today will challenge us to continue moving toward where God wants us to be in spite of limitations and obstacles in our lives. We must believe that God will protect and provide for us even in the most desperate of circumstances. We who are the body of Christ can take notes from the United States Postal Service creed: "Neither snow nor rain nor heat nor gloom of night stays these couriers from the swift completion of their appointed rounds." God has appointed rounds for us, and we cannot be late for our appointment with our destiny.

SCRIPTURE VOCABULARY

Potiphar—He was an Egyptian officer and captain of the guard who bought Joseph from the Ishmaelites. Potiphar gave Joseph charge over the care of his household. This name, Potiphar, signifies one "devoted to the sun."

Ishmaelites—According to the biblical record, the Ishmaelites were a nomadic people and descendants of Ishmael, the son of Abraham and the elder half-brother of Isaac. The Ishmaelites sold Joseph to Potiphar.

SCRIPTURE REFERENCE

Genesis 39:1–6, 16–23

Genesis 39:1–6

1 Now Joseph had been taken down to Egypt. And Potiphar, an officer of Pharaoh, captain of the guard, an Egyptian, bought him from the Ishmaelites who had taken him down there.

2 The Lord was with Joseph, and he was a successful man; and he was in the house of his master the Egyptian.

3 And his master saw that the Lord was with him and that the Lord made all he did to prosper in his hand.

4 So Joseph found favor in his sight, and served him. Then he made him overseer of his house, and all that he had he put under his authority.

5 So it was, from the time that he had made him overseer of his house and all that he had, that the Lord blessed the

Egyptian's house for Joseph's sake; and the blessing of the Lord was on all that he had in the house and in the field.

6 Thus he left all that he had in Joseph's hand, and he did not know what he had except for the bread which he ate. Now Joseph was handsome in form and appearance.

Genesis 39:16–23

16 So she kept his garment with her until his master came home.

17 Then she spoke to him with words like these, saying, "The Hebrew servant whom you brought to us came in to me to mock me;

18 so it happened, as I lifted my voice and cried out, that he left his garment with me and fled outside."

19 So it was, when his master heard the words which his wife spoke to him, saying, "Your servant did to me after this manner," that his anger was aroused.

20 Then Joseph's master took him and put him into the prison, a place where the king's prisoners were confined. And he was there in the prison.

21 But the Lord was with Joseph and showed him mercy, and He gave him favor in the sight of the keeper of the prison.

22 And the keeper of the prison committed to Joseph's hand all the prisoners who were in the prison; whatever they did there, it was his doing.

23 The keeper of the prison did not look into anything that was under Joseph's authority, because the Lord was with him; and whatever he did, the Lord made it prosper.

MEMORY VERSE

Thou madest him to have dominion over the works of thy hands; thou has put all things under his feet (Psalm 8:6).

HOW DOES THE MEMORY VERSE APPLY TO YOUR SPIRITUAL LIFE?

_____

_____

_____

_____

_____

_____

_____

LESSON FOCUS

God has a plan for His believers, even when it seems the odds are stacked against us. As believers of Christ, our mission is to keep walking in the faith that God will provide for us and direct us where He wants us to be. In light of those who would stop or hinder our progress in traveling where God wants us to be, ours is not to be pessimistic, fearful, or doubtful of God's faithfulness.

BIBLE BACKGROUND

Joseph was second youngest of Jacob's 12 sons (the only one younger was Benjamin). However, Jacob had a special relationship with Joseph; in fact, the Bible says that Jacob loved Joseph more than all his other children. Because he loved him so, Jacob made Joseph a beautiful multicolored coat. Joseph's brothers saw the coat and hated him even more. Then Joseph made the situation more strained. He had two dreams, both inferring that he would have dominion over his brothers; again their hatred intensified.

A few days later, Joseph's father asked him to check on his brothers in the fields quite a distance away. Joseph went to find them. When the brothers saw him in the distance, they made a plan to kill him. However, when Reuben, Joseph's oldest brother, heard this, he said, "Let's not kill him; just throw him in a well out here in the field." He secretly planned to rescue Joseph when the other brothers had left.

So when Joseph arrived, they took off his multicolored robe and threw him in an empty well. A little while later, a group known as the Ishmaelites came by wanting to sell some things in Egypt. One of the brothers spoke up: "Why don't we sell him to these people? This way we never have to see him again, and we don't have to kill him." The other brothers agreed and sold him to the Ishamelites. Unfortunately, Reuben hadn't seen what happened. When he returned to the well, he noticed that Joseph was gone. The rest of the brothers took Joseph's robe, dipped it in animal blood, and took it back to their father. When Jacob saw this, he cried, "Some animal has killed my son," and mourned Joseph's death.

While in Egypt, Joseph started out as a slave, sold to Potiphar, an Egyptian officer and captain of the guard for the Pharaoh of Egypt. However, the Lord was with Joseph and gave him favor. So Potiphar made him his helper, and put him in charge of everything that he owned.

The problem came when Potiphar's wife lied about Joseph to her husband and had him thrown into jail. The Lord was still with Joseph in jail, and the warden put him in charge of all the prisoners. Joseph never worried because the Lord was with him and helped him do everything right.

SCRIPTURE EXPLORATION
Genesis 39:1–6, 16–23

In today's Scripture, Joseph was sold into slavery, taken to Egypt, and became manager of Potiphar's household until Potiphar's wife falsely accused him and had him thrown in prison. This was the opposite of how Joseph grew up. He was the center of his father's attention with many opportunities for a successful life. However, because of his brothers' hatred and jealousy, his life changed immensely, but God allowed Joseph to be directed to his destiny.

Genesis 39:1–6

¹ *Now Joseph had been taken down to Egypt. And Potiphar, an officer of Pharaoh, captain of the guard, an Egyptian, bought him from the Ishmaelites who had taken him down there.*

² *The Lord was with Joseph, and he was a successful man; and he was in the house of his master the Egyptian.*

³ *And his master saw that the Lord was with him and that the Lord made all he did to prosper in his hand.*

⁴ *So Joseph found favor in his sight, and served him. Then he made him overseer of his house, and all that he had he put under his authority.*

⁵ *So it was, from the time that he had made him overseer of his house and all that he had, that the Lord blessed the Egyptian's house for Joseph's sake; and the blessing of the Lord was on all that he had in the house and in the field.*

⁶ *Thus he left all that he had in Joseph's hand, and he did not know what he had except for the bread which he ate. Slaves captured in war were generally sent to labor in the field and subjected to hard treatment by taskmasters. However, those bought with money—such as Joseph—were*

employed in homes and treated kindly, and enjoyed some liberties.

When Joseph was taken to Egypt, he was sold to Potiphar, an officer of Pharaoh, captain of the guard, and an Egyptian by birth. He was a trusted person in Pharaoh's court, and as such, he was well connected and could get the best of everything, including slaves. Even in a place where Joseph was not known, the fact that God was with him and did not abandon him provides stability. God's presence with him was never interrupted, staying with him in a new and fearful environment. Moreover, he is successful because he is connected to God.

Joseph's success comes not only from God but also from his relationship with Potiphar. Of all the people who could have bought him, Joseph becomes the manager of Potiphar's affairs. Potiphar's power and position produce an opportunity for Joseph to become well-known, even in his prison experience. Perhaps it was said when he arrived in prison, "Joseph managed Potiphar's household, and word on the streets is he did a great job." Joseph's relationship with Potiphar gives him presence and notoriety in a foreign land and entry to a place where he will experience emotional, psychological, and spiritual pain.

God made sure Joseph advanced in his position, even as a slave. Joseph finds favor in Potiphar's eyes and not only serves him but also takes charge of his household. Although Joseph was a slave, he did not let his status in life determine his attitude nor limit him from doing his best. Because of his commitment to his position, Joseph becomes a blessing to the entire household. He allows God to use him as a positive change agent in Potiphar's affairs. Because Potiphar recognized Joseph's competence, he placed everything he had in Joseph's hands. Potiphar received more than he thought a slave could provide.

Genesis 39:16–23

16 *So she kept his garment with her until his master came home.*

17 *Then she spoke to him with words like these, saying, "The Hebrew servant whom you brought to us came in to me to mock me;*

18 *so it happened, as I lifted my voice and cried out, that he left his garment with me and fled outside."*

19 *So it was, when his master heard the words which his wife spoke to him, saying, "Your servant did to me after this manner," that his anger was aroused.*

20 *Then Joseph's master took him and put him into the prison, a place where the king's prisoners were confined. And he was there in the prison.*

21 *But the Lord was with Joseph and showed him mercy, and He gave him favor in the sight of the keeper of the prison.*

22 *And the keeper of the prison committed to Joseph's hand all the prisoners who were in the prison; whatever they did there, it was his doing.*

23 *The keeper of the prison did not look into anything that was under Joseph's authority, because the Lord was with him; and whatever he did, the Lord made it prosper.*

Potiphar's wife endeavored to have Joseph by any means necessary; when he rebuffed her, she decided to falsely accuse him of assaulting her. In telling her husband, Potiphar's wife did not mention Joseph's name as the assailant, instead referring to him as "the Hebrew servant." Mentioning his name would give him value, but not mentioning his name would treat him as chattel that misbehaved and must be punished.

After hearing his wife's words and seeing the torn garment, Potiphar became angry and threw Joseph into prison. However, why didn't Potiphar injure or kill Joseph if he believed his wife's accusation? Perhaps he did not believe her, but in an effort to assuage the situation, he came up with a nonlethal punishment. Joseph was put in prison, although he had not committed a crime. He suffered the injustice that many experience today—being wrongly accused of a crime they did not commit.

However, the Lord was still with Joseph and showed him mercy. Again, Joseph was given favor, and as a result, the keeper of the prison was so impressed that he put Joseph in charge. Just like with Potiphar, the keeper of the prison had nothing to worry about. Joseph was protected and blessed by God; his destiny was not to remain a slave or die prematurely because of his brothers or former master's wife. God had a plan and a purpose for Joseph that would be fulfilled. What plan does God have for you that is blocked by obstacles? How are you responding to the obstacles you cannot overcome without additional help or resources?

DISCUSSION

1. List some of the characteristics Joseph had that helped him to maintain his disposition even when being lied about.

2. When people label you or place you in a specific "box," how do you respond?

3. How do you continue to trust God at times when it feels like more "bad than good" is happening to you?

PRACTICAL APPLICATION

PERSONAL APPLICATION

1. Have you ever been accused of something you did not do? If so, did you lose your job or standing in the community, and what did you do to rectify the situation?

2. What specific things can you do to help encourage a fellow church member or neighbor who feels like everything is going wrong for them?

COMMUNITY APPLICATION

1. Is there a project that your church can do to encourage people in the community to believe that their situation can get better?

_____

_____

_____

_____

_____

_____

_____

_____

_____

_____

2. How can you bring the light of Christ to a secular organization that helps the hurting people in your community? Consider the many different ways you could show love by doing a search on your city's website of social groups that meet regularly.

_____

_____

_____

_____

_____

_____

_____

_____

_____

_____

_____

MEDITATION

We can feel the presence of God in many ways. As we face our days, sometimes stressed and anxious, we need only look toward the sun's rays to feel God's warmth; walk outside and encounter His presence in the gentle breeze swirling around us; and stand still in one of the many moments He grants us. In every moment, we can feel assured that even when we don't feel God's presence, He is always with us. If we know and feel this with all of our being, the life that God has in store for us is within our reach.

PRAYER

Dear Heavenly Father,
We pray for belief and trust in You even in our uncertainty of purpose and moments of darkness. We pray that we will recognize and reflect upon Your steadfast consistency in our lives. We pray for the power to continue our worship and praise for You even when we don't feel like it. Forgive us for the moments we want to give up on both You and ourselves. Help us to be people of persistence, consistency, and courage as we continue to witness to all regarding the love of Christ. Thank You, Father, and we welcome You to continue to abide with us. Amen.

BIBLIOGRAPHY

http://www.studylight.org/commentaries/jfb/view.cgi?bk=ge&ch=39#1. (Accessed July 24th, 2014.)

http://www.dltk-bible.com/genesis/story_of_joseph-cv.htm. (Accessed July 24th, 2014.)

http://www.enduringword.com/commentaries/0139.htm. (Accessed July 26th, 2014.)

https://www.biblegateway.com/passage/?search=genesis+39&version=KJV. (Accessed July 26th, 2014.)

CHAPTER 2

MAKING A BOLD MOVE

SCRIPTURE LESSON

Numbers 27:1–11

BACKGROUND SCRIPTURES

Numbers 15:32–36, 26:53, 27:33, 36:1–12; Deuteronomy 25:5–10; Joshua 17:3–4;
Psalm 8:23, 60:67; Galatians 3:28

QUESTION

What does it mean for Christians to make bold moves? As persecution for taking a stand for Christ continues to build, what is our response? We could "go along to get along" and not make any waves so that no one feels uncomfortable. Or we could stand up for what is right in making bold steps of faith for the kingdom of God. A bold step for Christ isn't for cowards. It's for those who are filled with the Holy Spirit and willing to follow His promptings at whatever the cost. Are you ready to be bold for Christ?

BE BOLD OR BE QUIET!

One of the most prolific and boldest activists during the Civil Rights Movement was Mrs. Fannie Lou Hamer. She was the youngest of 20 children and worked most of her life on a plantation. Fannie went in for a minor surgical procedure; however, afterward she discovered the doctor had performed a hysterectomy without her consent. At that time, many African American women were unjustly sterilized by their doctors, and this life-transforming event compelled Fannie to work toward civil rights.

On the same day Fannie registered to vote, she and her entire family were fired from their jobs. She went on to take part in the Mississippi Freedom Summer with the Student Nonviolent Coordinating Committee in 1962. As a result of her civil rights work, Fannie was brutally beaten, shot at, and threatened with bodily harm. None of these caused her to stop the work because she was resolute in her bold convictions of dealing with injustice.

When other workers were feeling nervous or afraid, Fannie would comfort them with Christian hymns. She became widely known when she spoke at the Democratic National Convention about her personal suffering due to the denial of her civil rights. Her passionate and compelling testimony opened the eyes of many Americans about the injustice of laws against African Americans.

For every one "Fannie Lou Hamer," there were probably hundreds of people who were afraid to stand up for what was right. They didn't want to lose their jobs or risk personal safety; however, Fannie's bold determination set her apart from all the others who didn't have her courage. Just like Fannie, you have the opportunity to be bold in your faith so that the Good News is preached to the world. You can be bold and ready to take on the challenge, or you can be quiet and never make a mark in building the kingdom of God. The choice is yours!

DISCUSSION

Fannie's suffering propelled her to be bold at a time when her life and livelihood were at risk. We also may find our courage in times of distress and trials. What life experiences have compelled you to stand up and be bold? Would you have moved in this situation if there weren't a painful experience? How does the Lord equip His people to be bold in troubling times?

TRANSITION

Our lesson challenges each of us to stand up with boldness amid difficulties. God has called His people to be strong and courageous in spite of the threat of trials and tragedies. Each believer is well equipped through prayer, Bible study, and Christian fellowship to be the bold person God has called for His purposes.

SCRIPTURE VOCABULARY

Korah—He was a Levite who along with two other men stirred up dissension against Moses and Aaron. They opposed Moses because they were dissatisfied with how positions of authority were set up. As a result, Moses prayed and God made a unique judgment in which all the conspirators were swallowed up alive into the ground or burned alive with fire (Numbers 16).

Inheritance—Land inherited as a result of God's promise to the Israelites was a significant responsibility among families. No inheritance could pass between the tribes of Israel. The firstborn son received the largest portion and had the responsibility to divide the inheritance with other family members. Because of his greater portion, the firstborn son had to also provide for his mother and sisters until their marriage or death.

SCRIPTURE REFERENCE

Numbers 27:1–11
1 Then came the daughters of

Zelophehad, the son of Hepher, the son of Gilead, the son of Machir, the son of Manasseh, of the families of Manasseh the son of Joseph: and these are the names of his daughters; Mahlah, Noah, and Hoglah, and Milcah, and Tirzah.

2 And they stood before Moses, and before Eleazar the priest, and before the princes and all the congregation, by the door of the tabernacle of the congregation, saying,

3 Our father died in the wilderness, and he was not in the company of them that gathered themselves together against the LORD in the company of Korah; but died in his own sin, and had no sons.

4 Why should the name of our father be done away from among his family, because he hath no son? Give unto us therefore a possession among the brethren of our father.

5 And Moses brought their cause before the LORD.

6 And the LORD spake unto Moses, saying,

7 The daughters of Zelophehad speak right: thou shalt surely give them a possession of an inheritance among their father's brethren; and thou shalt cause the inheritance of their father to pass unto them.

8 And thou shalt speak unto the children of Israel, saying, If a man die, and have no son, then ye shall cause his inheritance to pass unto his daughter.

9 And if he have no daughter, then ye shall give his inheritance unto his brethren.

10 And if he have no brethren, then ye shall give his inheritance unto his father's brethren.

11 And if his father have no brethren, then ye shall give his inheritance unto his kinsman that is next to him of his family, and he shall possess it: and it shall be unto the children of Israel a statute of judgment, as the LORD commanded Moses.

MEMORY VERSE

Seeing then that we have such hope, we use great plainness of speech (from 2 Corinthians 3:12).

HOW DOES THE MEMORY VERSE APPLY TO YOUR SPIRITUAL LIFE?

_____

_____

_____

_____

_____

_____

LESSON FOCUS

The main idea of this lesson is that believers of the Lord Jesus Christ are called to be bold and courageous just like the daughters of Zelophehad. Our boldness stems from the stirring up of our hearts through the Holy Spirit. The life of a Christian isn't one of shrinking back from controversy or situations, but rather a bold and solid stand in faith.

BIBLE BACKGROUND

When Moses and the Israelites left Egypt, it was assumed that everyone who left would eventually enter the Promised Land. However, because of the grumblings of the people, everyone over the age of 20 was excluded, with the exception of Joshua and Caleb (Numbers 27:14–32). Moses was kept from entering the land due to his disobedience in hitting the rock instead of speaking to it as the Lord commanded him (Numbers 20:1–13).

The Israelites traveled in the wilderness for forty years, until the last person who had been more than 20 years old died.

A census was done to count the people in determining the division of the Promised Land. Women weren't counted as a part of the census or in the distribution of land. Zelophehad died in the wilderness, leaving his five daughters without a brother, and therefore without any inheritance in the Promised Land. These women needed to step up and boldly speak out so that their families would be taken care of in the future.

SCRIPTURE EXPLORATION

Numbers 27:1–2

It was a time of transition for the nation of Israel when Zelophehad's daughters approached Moses. The Israelites were preparing to find their long-anticipated homeland. Zelophehad's daughters didn't start a controversy or rebellion against Moses. Rather, they followed proper protocol by speaking directly to Moses, Elezar the priest, and the leaders of the clans, with the congregation present.

Their request was significant for the continuation of their family to be counted among the tribes of Israel. After Moses prayed, God supported the request of the daughters of Zelophehad and established a statute for the Israelites to follow when dealing with inherited land. Later, the chief fathers of the tribe approached Moses to make sure Zelophehad's daughters only married within their tribe. Moses declared that they were allowed to share in the inheritance as long as they married within their own clan. If they chose to marry into another tribe, they would lose their inheritance because inherited land couldn't be transferred between tribes.

This statute of judgment was significant because it established protection of future families and the rights of women. Zelophehad's daughters also revealed their faith in God because the land wasn't yet conquered. In faith, they believed that God would give them the ability to overcome and live on the land with their families.

¹ *Then came the daughters of Zelophehad, the son of Hepher, the son of Gilead, the son of Machir, the son of Manasseh, of the families of Manasseh the son of Joseph: and these are the names of his daughters; Mahlah, Noah, and Hoglah, and Milcah, and Tirzah.*

When Joseph was on his deathbed, he made the Children of Israel promise that they would bring his bones to the Promised Land (Genesis 50:25, Exodus 13:19). This was significant because Joseph believed in the promise made to his great-grandfather Abraham to his grandfather Isaac and finally through his father Jacob. At the time of Jacob's death, Joseph's sons Manasseh and Ephraim were counted along with Joseph's brothers as a part of the 12 tribes of Israel (Genesis 48:17–20).

Zelophehad's daughters' request was significant to keeping with the blessing of Joseph's sons and his continued inheritance in the Promised Land. God always keeps His promises, even when hundreds of years have passed. As believers, we can trust in God to keep His promises even when significant time has passed. God isn't like a person, who forgets, but rather He never fails to keep His word. In 2 Corinthians 1:20, we learn that "For no matter how many promises God has made, they are 'Yes' in Christ. And so through him the 'Amen' is spoken by us to the glory of God."

² *And they stood before Moses, and before Eleazar the priest, and before the princes and all the congregation, by the door of the tabernacle of the congregation, saying,*

After the Children of Israel escaped from Egypt, they needed to learn how to govern themselves under God's authority and not man's. From these former slaves, leaders and protocols were established for order. As God's chosen leader, Moses felt the pressure to deal with every great and small issue. It was Jethro, Moses' father-in-law, who advised him to set up God-fearing, wise, and capable leaders to share the burden (Exodus 28:21–26).

God established laws in order for Israel to be a nation that follows a theocracy—a nation and government that followed God, not men. In the matter of Zelophehad's daughters' request, they needed to speak directly to Moses as the land inheritance was an important and vital issue for the Israelites. Unlike Korah, they didn't question Moses' authority or God's choice of a leader. In turn, Moses prayed to God for an ultimate answer rather than seeking the counsel of his peers.

Numbers 27:3–4
³ *Our father died in the wilderness, and he was not in the company of them that gathered themselves together against the LORD in the company of Korah; but died in his own sin, and had no sons.*

⁴ *Why should the name of our father be done away from among his family, because he hath no son? Give unto us therefore a possession among the brethren of our father.*

It was important for Zelophehad's daughters to establish that their father wasn't a part of Korah's rebellion. As the nation of Israel traveled 40 years in the wilderness, they struggled with walking in complete obedience to God. They murmured against Moses many times, even threatening his life (Exodus 17:4). They went out for manna on the Sabbath when the Lord commanded them not to do it (Exodus 16:20, 27), made an idol calf when Moses was with the Lord, complained in God's presence (Numbers 11:1), and rebelled because of the spies' report (Numbers 13:31).

The Lord punished quickly those who rebelled against the truth and caused others to rebel as well. We live in the age of grace because of the sacrifice of Jesus; however, God doesn't change and He will punish those who rebel against the truth. Christians must always check their hearts to be sure that they are living a life that is pleasing and obedient to the Lord (2 Corinthians 13:5).

Numbers 27:5–7
5 *And Moses brought their cause before the LORD.*

6 *And the LORD spake unto Moses, saying,*

7 *The daughters of Zelophehad speak right: thou shalt surely give them a possession of an inheritance among their father's brethren; and thou shalt cause the inheritance of their father to pass unto them.*

Because women had less authority than men in the Hebrew culture, the Lord set up His laws to protect them. Both boys and girls were believed to be gifts from God, which set their culture apart from the pagans. Fathers and brothers had the responsibility to make sure the women in their family had everything they needed for survival (Deuteronomy 22:13–19).

In 1 Timothy 5:8, Paul writes that "anyone who does not provide for their relatives, and especially for their own household, has denied the faith and is worse than an unbeliever" (NIV). The Lord hears the prayers of the widow and fatherless. The body of Christ has the responsibility to take care of our spiritual family members when their natural family won't or is unable to care for them.

Numbers 27:8–11
8 *And thou shalt speak unto the children of Israel, saying, If a man die, and have no son, then ye shall cause his inheritance to pass unto his daughter.*

9 *And if he have no daughter, then ye shall give his inheritance unto his brethren.*

10 *And if he have no brethren, then ye shall give his inheritance unto his father's brethren.*

11 *And if his father have no brethren, then ye shall give his inheritance unto his kinsman that is next to him of his family, and he shall possess it: and it shall be unto the children of Israel a statute of judgment, as the LORD commanded Moses.*

Zelophehad's daughters' request was bigger than just their specific need. By boldly coming forward, they helped establish a statute for all women who didn't have a male relative to protect them. From their request, a long line of circumstances were addressed keeping the inherited land in the family line. This was the especially significant principle in the marriage of Boaz to Ruth the Moabitess. Boaz had to seek the permission of the closest relative before he could marry Ruth. This relative gave Boaz the right to marry Ruth because he wanted to protect his own family inheritance (Ruth 4:5–6). As a result, the inheritance of Naomi's husband and sons were preserved. The greater beauty was that Boaz and Ruth had a son, Obed, leading to the birth of Israel's King David, leading to the birth of Christ Jesus (Ruth 4:22, Matthew 1:5).

We can never underestimate God's plan for our lives and stepping up in bold moves for the faith. Whatever our issue or problem, the Lord knows how to turn it for good (Romans 8:28). It's tempting to think that our dilemmas are just about us and don't affect the generation that comes after us. It's critical that we take a stand for the Lord and trust in Him to lead the next generation in the right paths.

2. Moses responded to their request with immediately praying to God for clarity. How does this set the example for leaders in the church looking for answers to problems?

3. Their request resulted in a legal requirement in the nation of Israel so that no family would be without an inheritance. Looking back on God's promise to Abraham in Genesis 12:2 and 15:18, why was this statute significant?

PRACTICAL APPLICATION

PERSONAL APPLICATION

1. Have you even been compelled to make a bold move in your faith? What was the consequence of it? How do you decipher between a bold move in faith or in fear?

2. The purpose of the inherited land was to prepare for the future needs of the next generation. What plans have you invested spiritually, emotionally, or physically for the generation following after you?

DISCUSSION

1. Zelophehad's daughters were faced with potentially losing their father's inheritance. Why do you think it was necessary for them to point out how he died in the wilderness?

COMMUNITY APPLICATION

1. Unfortunately, women still struggle around the world. Are there widows in your church? How does your ministry provide and care for widows? What about the single mothers who are struggling? How does your church reach out to assist single parents in general?

_____

_____

_____

_____

_____

2. Many unbelievers come to Christ as a result of being shown Christian compassion and love. Are there opportunities in your ministry to help hurting people get back on their feet after tragedies?

_____

_____

_____

_____

_____

MEDITATION

Secular culture demonstrates a boldness that isn't of God—most demonstrated on TV reality shows. However, the boldness that comes from the Holy Spirit is controlled, peaceful, and unafraid of what man can do. As followers of Jesus Christ, we need to stand up and speak the truth in love—that God sent His only Son to die for the sins of the world. There is much unrest and sadness in the world, but the bold proclamations of God's people can bring healing and restoration. Meditate on what the Holy Spirit is stirring up in your heart to make a difference in the lives of those around you.

PRAYER

Dear Heavenly Father,
You are a faithful God who keeps Your promises. Forgive us for the times we doubted Your love for us and succumbed to fear instead of faith. Build us up in our spirits to follow Your precepts with a pure heart and a bold stance. Help us to speak up when You open up the opportunity to share our faith. We trust in Your guidance. In Jesus' name, amen.

BIBLIOGRAPHY

Keener, Craig S. *The IVP Bible Background Commentary New Testament*. Downers Grove, Illinois: InterVarsity Press, 1993. 675.

Packer, J. I., Tenney, Merrill C., and White Jr., William. *Illustrated Encyclopedia of Bible Facts*. Nashville, Tennessee: Thomas Nelson Publishers, 1995. 378–395, 412–431.

Unger, Merrill F. *The New Unger's Bible Dictionary*. Chicago: Moody Press, 1957. 929.

Walvoord, John F. and Roy B. Zuck. *The Bible Knowledge Commentary*. Colorado Springs, C: Chariot Victor Publishing, 1985. 247.

https://www.biblegateway.com/passage/?search= numbers+27&version=KJV. Accessed July 19, 2014.

http://www.biography.com/people/fannie-lou-hamer-20562. Accessed July 19, 2014.

http://www.nwhm.org/education-resources/ biography/biographies/fannie-lou-hamer/. Accessed July 19, 2014.

http://www.pbs.org/wgbh/americanexperience/ features/biography/freedomsummer-hammer. Accessed July 19, 2014.

NOTES

CHAPTER 3

INTERCESSORY PRAYER MEETING

SCRIPTURE LESSON

2 Kings 19:14–21, 25–36

BACKGROUND SCRIPTURES

Isaiah 37:14–38

QUESTION

What prompts you to pray an intercessory prayer? Think about a time when you were moved to stop and call a prayer meeting on behalf of an emergency, a sudden illness, or accident.

PRAYER TIME

On a hot, muggy July Sunday morning in a small rural church, there was no air conditioning unit working, and a hot breeze was blowing through the open windows. The two large floor fans, one in the front and one in the back of the church, did not provide adequate cooling for the sweltering summer heat. To add to their misery, the fans were set at a low speed so the congregation could hear the guest pastor's prayers and sermon.

After reading the Scripture, praying, and beginning his sermon introduction, Rev. Jerald Green noticed one of the men in the congregation, sitting on the fifth pew from the front of church, slumped forward. At first, Rev. Green thought the man was bowing in prayer. Then, he noticed that the man's wife was trying to hold him up and others were trying to help her; some people were frantically waving their hands to get Rev. Green's attention.

Rev. Green finally realized something was wrong with the man, and stopped preaching. He sprung down the steps from the pulpit and ran to the man, who was having difficulty breathing. Rev. Green asked everyone to join him in prayer for the man's recovery. While the guest pastor and the congregation prayed, someone called for an ambulance, and the organist played a hymn very softly. In about 10–12 minutes, the ambulance arrived with emergency medical personnel who assisted the man before they carried him and his wife to the hospital.

Ten years later, Rev. Green was invited back to the church for the church anniversary. One of the deacons was still telling everyone about the time Rev. Green ran from the pulpit and held an intercessory prayer meeting on behalf of one of their members, Mr. Brown, in the midst of his sermon. Rev. Green smiled and nodded his head as he heard the story. He was happy to see Mr. Brown as they greeted each other. At the end of the story, Mr. Brown said, "Thank you, Reverend, and thank You, Jesus."

DISCUSSION

In view of the seriousness of the situation, what would you have done if someone tried to get your attention for help in the midst of your pastor's sermon? Explain what you would have done and why.

TRANSITION

We see in this story that a prayer meeting was certainly in order because of the dire situation. When King Hezekiah received a threatening letter from Sennacherib, who questioned his resources and tried to strike fear into Hezekiah's faith in God for deliverance, Hezekiah prayed to God.

He also sent a delegation to the priest, Isaiah, to brief him on the emergency situation.

Hezekiah realized that God's power and name had been blasphemed.

SCRIPTURE VOCABULARY

Hezekiah—The 12th king of Judah, ascended the throne at age 25 and reigned for 29 years; one of three very good kings of Judah.

Sennacherib—Assyrian ruler from 705–681 B.C. that threatened King Hezekiah. The prophet Isaiah prophesied Sennacherib's fall.

Assyria—Kingdom founded by Asshur and Nimrod (Genesis 2:14) and fought against Judah (2 Kings 18:9; Isaiah 36:1).

Cherubim—Angelic creature (Exodus 37:9; 1 Samuel 4:4; 2 Chronicles 3:11–13; Psalm 80:1; Ezekiel 1:10).

SCRIPTURE REFERENCE

2 Kings 19:14–21
14 And Hezekiah received the letter of the hand of the messengers, and read it: and Hezekiah went up into the house of the LORD, and spread it before the LORD.

15 And Hezekiah prayed before the LORD, and said, O LORD God of Israel, which dwellest between the cherubims, thou art the God, even thou alone, of

all the kingdoms of the earth; thou hast made heaven and earth.

16 LORD, bow down thine ear, and hear: open, LORD, thine eyes, and see: and hear the words of Sennacherib, which hath sent him to reproach the living God.

17 Of a truth, LORD, the kings of Assyria have destroyed the nations and their lands,

18 And have cast their gods into the fire: for they were no gods, but the work of men's hands, wood and stone: therefore they have destroyed them.

19 Now therefore, O LORD our God, I beseech thee, save thou us out of his hand, that all the kingdoms of the earth may know that thou art the LORD God, even thou only.

20 Then Isaiah the son of Amoz sent to Hezekiah, saying, Thus saith the LORD God of Israel, That which thou hast prayed to me against Sennacherib king of Assyria I have heard.

21 This is the word that the LORD hath spoken concerning him; The virgin the daughter of Zion hath despised thee, and laughed thee to scorn; the daughter of Jerusalem hath shaken her head at thee.

2 Kings 19:25–36

25 Hast thou not heard long ago how I have done it, and of ancient times that I have formed it? now have I brought it to pass, that thou shouldest be to lay waste fenced cities into ruinous heaps.

26 Therefore their inhabitants were of small power, they were dismayed and confounded; they were as the grass of the field, and as the green herb, as the grass on the housetops, and as corn blasted before it be grown up.

27 But I know thy abode, and thy going out, and thy coming in, and thy rage against me.

28 Because thy rage against me and thy tumult is come up into mine ears, therefore I will put my hook in thy nose, and my bridle in thy lips, and I will turn thee back by the way by which thou camest.

29 And this shall be a sign unto thee, Ye shall eat this year such things as grow of themselves, and in the second year that which springeth of the same; and in the third year sow ye, and reap, and plant vineyards, and eat the fruits thereof.

30 And the remnant that is escaped of the house of Judah shall yet again take root downward, and bear fruit upward.

31 For out of Jerusalem shall go forth a remnant, and they that escape out of mount Zion: the zeal of the LORD of hosts shall do this.

32 Therefore thus saith the LORD concerning the king of Assyria, He shall not come into this city, nor shoot an arrow there, nor come before it with shield, nor cast a bank against it.

33 By the way that he came, by the same

shall he return, and shall not come into this city, saith the LORD.

34 For I will defend this city, to save it, for mine own sake, and for my servant David's sake.

35 And it came to pass that night that the angel of the LORD went out, and smote in the camp of the Assyrians an hundred fourscore and five thousand: and when they arose early in the morning, behold, they were all dead corpses.

36 So Sennacherib king of Assyria departed, and went and returned, and dwelt at Nineveh.

MEMORY VERSE

God is our refuge and strength, a very present help in trouble (Psalm 46:1).

HOW DOES THE MEMORY VERSE APPLY TO YOUR SPIRITUAL LIFE?

_____

_____

_____

_____

_____

_____

LESSON FOCUS

This lesson focuses on Hezekiah's prayer and the work of Isaiah the priest, who delivers God's answer to the prophet Hezekiah.

BIBLE BACKGROUND

The second book of Kings is a continuation of the former giving account of Israel's history from Ahaziah's reign to the Assyrian destruction of Samaria, the capital of the Northern kingdom. The book of 2 Kings also contains the reign of Jehoshaphat, the fall of Jerusalem and the Babylonian exile. Hezekiah's reign (715-686 BC) is a high point in Judah's history because he is the first king to walk in the ways of David (HarperCollins Study Bible, 2006, 519).

The purpose of 2 Kings is to show how those who are unwilling to follow God and do not allow Him to lead them face a different final destiny unlike those who choose Him. Although the author of 2 Kings is not known, the prophet Jeremiah has been noted as a possible author or maybe even several other prophets (Life Application Bible, 546). The writer or writers of 2 Kings wanted the Children of Israel to know how idolatry and following others' ways leads to destruction. The relationship between God and the people would be strained and torn because of how the people wanted to live for other gods.

One of the major characters in 1 Kings is the prophet Elijah. Elijah's ministry through his death is carried on in 2

Kings. He was constantly challenging and fighting against the wickedness of leaders who were against God and His people. Elijah prophesied and fought against idolatry for fifty years. He challenged the people to return to God and follow His statutes . During this time, Elijah performed many miracles through the power of God, i.e., in 1 Kings 1:9–14, Elijah calls for fire to destroy the captains and their men because they were not sincere in calling Elijah "man of God," or the parting of the Jordan River as both Elijah and Elisha were ready to cross (2 Kings 2:6–8). Elijah was a man of power and a great prophet. After Elijah's fiery chariot ride home to heaven, Elisha was given Elijah's mantle to preach against idolatry and to remind the people of God's call to serve Him only.

The book of 2 Kings is divided into two sections—chapters 1–17 represents the divided kingdom and chapters 18–25 represents the surviving kingdom. Although the Northern Kingdom had been desolated, Josiah and Hezekiah were both able to help fight against the wicked ways that dominated God's people. Both kings were able to repair the temple and have the people come together for the Passover, and Josiah was able to remove all idolatry from the country (Life Application Bible, 547).

SCRIPTURE EXPLORATION

2 Kings 19:14–21

14 And Hezekiah received the letter of the hand of the messengers, and read it: and Hezekiah went up into the house of the LORD, and spread it before the LORD.

15 And Hezekiah prayed before the LORD, and said, O LORD God of Israel, which dwellest between the cherubims, thou art the God, even thou alone, of all the kingdoms of the earth; thou hast made heaven and earth.

16 LORD, bow down thine ear, and hear: open, LORD, thine eyes, and see: and hear the words of Sennacherib, which hath sent him to reproach the living God.

17 Of a truth, LORD, the kings of Assyria have destroyed the nations and their lands,

18 And have cast their gods into the fire: for they were no gods, but the work of men's hands, wood and stone: therefore they have destroyed them.

19 Now therefore, O LORD our God, I beseech thee, save thou us out of his hand, that all the kingdoms of the earth may know that thou art the LORD God, even thou only.

20 Then Isaiah the son of Amoz sent to Hezekiah, saying, Thus saith the LORD God of Israel, That which thou hast prayed to me against Sennacherib king of Assyria I have heard.

21 This is the word that the LORD hath spoken concerning him; The virgin the daughter of Zion hath despised thee, and

laughed thee to scorn; the daughter of Jerusalem hath shaken her head at thee.

Hezekiah realized that both God's power and His name had been blasphemed. So Hezekiah prayed a model prayer. He invoked the name of the Lord God of Israel, the covenant-keeping God who dwells between the cherubim, a symbolical creature (man, ox, lion, and eagle) representing His province among men, with the four faces expressing the characters of wisdom and intelligence, strength, kingly authority, and swiftness and farsightedness. He said that God alone made heaven and earth. Hezekiah prayed for God to "hear, open his eyes and see what Sennacherib has done to mock the living God" (2 Kings 19:16). After acknowledging who God is, where He dwells and His attributes, Hezekiah then pleaded for God to save them so that the kingdoms of the earth will know that He is God alone. Isaiah sent messengers to Hezekiah with the answer, "Thus saith the Lord, Do not be afraid because of the words that you have heard." Isaiah said that God has heard the king's prayer and has a word for Sennacherib.

Hezekiah was the king of Judah. He focused on making changes to the religious and civil disciplines in the lives of the people. His relationship with God was strong and he was able to push through the reforms needed to change the wicked's stronghold on the land. Hezekiah had a very strong prayer life that allowed him to stay focused on God, and listen to Him in many situations.

Hezekiah did not take God for granted. He knew that God had all power and could change the situation, but he was humbled to come before the Lord. He acknowledges what God alone can do and has done in spite of what the idolatrous worshipers have done to their phony gods. In verses 17–18, Hezekiah states, "Of a truth, LORD, the kings of Assyria have destroyed the nations and their lands, And have cast their gods into the fire: for they were no gods, but the work of men's hands, wood and stone: therefore they have destroyed them." The evil kings of Assyria have destroyed what they believed in and worshiped. Their false handmade gods are no match for God, who is not made with human hands. Hezekiah wanted and needed the true and powerful God to do something and change things around. He did not want Sennacherib's challenge to prevail. The people were already living a life that was not pleasing before the Lord.

In verses 20–21, the prophet Isaiah addresses Hezekiah's deep concerns. Isaiah assures Hezekiah that the Lord has listened and has pronounced judgment against Sennacherib. God will not be mocked and has plans that will destroy what the wicked leader thought could not be touched by anyone or any power, including God.

In a sermon entitled How to Pray about Your Problems, Dr. Delman Coates said, "Get alone with God and pray first. Focus on God's attributes, not on your problem. Give up ownership of the problem. God has power over the problem." Dr. Coates said, "Prayer will help you cancel Satan's lies when the enemy tries to intimidate you with psychological warfare." In God's response to Hezekiah (2 Kings 19:21), He emphasizes that Jerusalem would not be violated by Sennacherib's boasting. God said that He "will put a hook through his nostrils and a muzzle on his lips and make him return back by the road he came" (2 Kings 19:28, New Jerusalem Bible).

2 Kings 19:25–36

25 *Hast thou not heard long ago how I have done it, and of ancient times that I have formed it? now have I brought it to pass, that thou shouldest be to lay waste fenced cities into ruinous heaps.*

26 *Therefore their inhabitants were of small power, they were dismayed and confounded; they were as the grass of the field, and as the green herb, as the grass on the housetops, and as corn blasted before it be grown up.*

27 *But I know thy abode, and thy going out, and thy coming in, and thy rage against me.*

28 *Because thy rage against me and thy tumult is come up into mine ears, therefore I will put my hook in thy nose, and my bridle in thy lips, and I will turn thee back by the way by which thou camest.*

29 *And this shall be a sign unto thee, Ye shall eat this year such things as grow of themselves, and in the second year that which springeth of the same; and in the*

third year sow ye, and reap, and plant vineyards, and eat the fruits thereof.

30 *And the remnant that is escaped of the house of Judah shall yet again take root downward, and bear fruit upward.*

31 *For out of Jerusalem shall go forth a remnant, and they that escape out of mount Zion: the zeal of the LORD of hosts shall do this.*

32 *Therefore thus saith the LORD concerning the king of Assyria, He shall not come into this city, nor shoot an arrow there, nor come before it with shield, nor cast a bank against it.*

33 *By the way that he came, by the same shall he return, and shall not come into this city, saith the LORD.*

34 *For I will defend this city, to save it, for mine own sake, and for my servant David's sake.*

35 *And it came to pass that night that the angel of the LORD went out, and smote in the camp of the Assyrians an hundred fourscore and five thousand: and when they arose early in the morning, behold, they were all dead corpses.*

36 *So Sennacherib king of Assyria departed, and went and returned, and dwelt at Nineveh.*

God confronted and questioned Sennacherib and asked him several rhetorical questions. Had he considered that his successes were foreordained by God? Had he considered that the people whom he had wreaked havoc on were totally powerless and helpless? Had he considered that God's divine government was at work and he was but an instrument of correction for Israel (Expositor's Bible Commentary, 1994, 568)?

In verses 25–36, God declares to Sennacherib that his efforts and works are nothing and will not stand because the Lord will destroy his empire. It was God who had allowed him to succeed, not his own work or insights. Hezekiah's dependence on God prevailed, not the threat of Sennacherib.

The Assyrians were known for treating their captives in very degrading, painful, and extremely harmful methods. An enslaved person would have a hook put in their nose. The Lord promised Sennacherib in verse 28 to do the same to the Assyrians: "Because thy rage against me and thy tumult is come up into mine ears, therefore I will put my hook in thy nose, and my bridle in thy lips, and I will turn thee back by the way by which thou camest." They would receive the same harsh treatment from God that they gave to others. The torment of "pulling off strips of skin until they [captured people] died" (Life Application Bible, 586) and other atrocities would no longer happen. God would repay them for the ruthless torture committed by the Assyrians, that Sennacherib indulged in and led.

God is in charge and knew all of the plans and details of Sennacherib's threats of destruction. Hezekiah received a symbolic guarantee that God's Word will come true, pointing to a three-year recovery plan for the surviving remnant. God turned to the immediate crisis; He will act for His own sake and for David's sake. God will always honor the covenant with the house of David despite spiritual and moral decay of Judah's kings (see 2 Kings 8:19; 2 Chronicles 21:7). God remains in control and His power cannot be undermined. God will act so that the kingdoms of the earth will know that He is God alone (Interpretation, First and Second Kings, A Bible Commentary for Teaching and Preaching, 1987, 240–242).

DISCUSSION

1. Why is the sequence of your name, your kingdom, and your will important in the prayer model?

2. When we pray "your kingdom come," what are we asking for?

PRACTICAL APPLICATION

PERSONAL APPLICATION

1. Use your contact list of friends and family members from your computer or smartphone and type a prayer from the Bible or one that you have written. Send a "Prayer a Day" for one week to the people on your contact list. Then watch how God works in your life and theirs.

2. Collect names from your church's prayer list of people who are sick, shut-in, or need special prayer, and pray for them. Ask your prayer partner or strong prayer warriors to join with you over the next month.

COMMUNITY APPLICATION

1. Seek the Lord's guidance on interceding on behalf of others who are in a crisis situation. Pray first, bring your plea before the Lord. Involve your Sunday School class, community, or church committee in prayer. Let God guide you into what to do.

2. Pray and work with community and church leaders to address issues that hurt and destroy lives in your community. Pray and work with others who may have insights and knowledge about the political and social structures of that particular concern or need.

MEDITATION

Lord, when our faith is under attack from the enemy's psychological warfare that would cause us to falter and give up, help us to focus on You, and Your attributes and power, not on the problem. Please help us to exercise complete faith and trust in Your wisdom and ability to deliver us from the enemy's attacks, whether it be a doctor's medical report, or any family or work crisis.

PRAYER

Dear Heavenly Father,
Sovereign God, Creator and Ruler of

heaven and earth, thank You for hearing our prayers and sending us the answers that we need in our times of crisis. We give You all the glory, honor, and praise. In Jesus' name we pray. Amen.

BIBLIOGRAPHY

Attridge, Harold W. General Editor. *HarperCollins Study Bible, Fully Revised and Updated, New Revised Standard Version*. New York, NY: HarperCollins Publishers, 2006.

Barker, Kenneth L. and John R. Kohlenberger III. *Expositor's Bible Commentary Abridged Edition, Old Testament*. Grand Rapids, Michigan: Zondervan Corp, 1994.

Coates, Delman. Excerpts from How to Pray About Your Problems, sermon. Mount Ennon Baptist Church, Clinton, Maryland, July 13, 2014.

Hartley, Fred, III. *Lord, Teach Us to Pray*. Colorado Springs, Colorado: NavPress, 2003. 47-48.

The Holy Bible, King James Version. Peabody, Massachusetts: Hendrickson Publishers, Inc., 2006.

Life Application Study Bible, NIV. Wheaton, Illinois and Grand Rapids, Michigan: Tyndale House Publishers, Inc. and Zondervan Publishing House, 1997. 546-547, 586.

Nelson, Richard D. *Interpretation, First and Second Kings: A Bible Commentary for Teaching and Preaching*. Louisville, KY: John Knox Press, 1987.

Smith, William, revised and edited by F.N. and M.A. Peloubet. *Smith's Bible Dictionary*. Nashville, Tennessee: Thomas Nelson Publishers, 1986.

Bible Explorer 3 Edition, King James Edition, 2 Kings 19:14-21, 25-36, July 2005-2006. Accessed July 1, 2014.

CHAPTER 4

GOD'S JUSTICE AND THE BURNING BUSH

SCRIPTURE LESSON
Exodus 3:1–10

BACKGROUND SCRIPTURES
Genesis 15:16, 43:32, 46:3–4, 32–34; Exodus 3:12, 19:1, 20–21;
Deuteronomy 33:16; Acts 7:30

QUESTION
How do you define justice? Share ways that you have defended someone who was bullied or treated unfairly by someone else. Has anyone stood up for you when you felt hopeless or unable to defend yourself or your family?

THE NEIGHBORHOOD HERO
Zach couldn't believe what had happened. The news reporters were asking him questions and the flashing lights were popping off. Zach saw the raging fire and smelled the strangling, black smoke erupting from his neighbor's house as he went outside to get the morning newspaper. Zach ran across the street shouting, "Fire, fire!" as he called 911. Zach dropped his phone as he tried to knock the door down, but it would not budge. He called out to his neighbors, but no reply. He ran around back and was able to climb through an open window that had smoke coming out. The smoke began to overtake him as he dropped to the ground and crawled. He heard someone crying and moved in that direction. By then, the sirens from the fire engines were shrieking down the street. Everyone had made it out safely through a side door except for one of the twins. He had fallen as the family ran outside, but as his mother and father turned around to run back for him, the fire and the smoke had become overwhelming, and they could not reach him. Zach struggled to crawl to where the cry came from. When he saw the twin, he miraculously was able to pick

up the twin and carry him. As Zach tried to make it back the way he came, a fireman headed into the house. He grabbed the child and called for help. A firewoman came to carry the twin as the fireman helped Zach to safety outside. Zach was a hero, even though he didn't think of himself that way or remember what happened. But, he was thankful to God that he was able to help!

DISCUSSION

Zach responded quickly in a time of crisis. He did not have time to think, just to act. How do you respond when someone needs your immediate help? Is there hesitation, fear, or an unwillingness to respond? Think about your responses over the years when a dangerous or crisis situation came in your life and make a list of the ways that you responded or not. Notice if there are any areas that you can change or redirect your responses in an emergency.

TRANSITION

God works in unexpected ways. The story of Moses and the burning bush demonstrates the power and awesome circumstances that God creates to make a difference for people and the world. God's justice for the people of Israel begins with a burning bush and a Hebrew, who was a former prince of the royal palace.

SCRIPTURE VOCABULARY

Moses—Moses was God's chosen person to deliver the Hebrew people from slavery in Egypt. He was raised as an Egyptian prince, but was born a Hebrew.

Jethro—Moses' wife Zipporah was the daughter of Jethro, who was a priest. He gave wise counsel to Moses that assisted him in leading the people.

Mount Horeb—Also known as Mount Sinai, it is the mountain where Moses meets God through the miraculous burning bush. Later, Moses would return to Mount Sinai and receive the Ten Commandments and other laws from God for the people to live by.

Midian—The land where Moses fled to after killing the Egyptian. Moses becomes a shepherd in Midian and marries Zipporah.

SCRIPTURE REFERENCE

Exodus 3:1–10
1 Now Moses kept the flock of Jethro his father in law, the priest of Midian: and he led the flock to the backside of the desert, and came to the mountain of God, even to Horeb.

2 And the angel of the LORD appeared unto him in a flame of fire out of the midst of a bush: and he looked, and, behold, the bush burned with fire, and the bush was not consumed.

3 And Moses said, I will now turn aside, and see this great sight, why the bush is not burnt.

4 And when the LORD saw that he turned aside to see, God called unto him out of the midst of the bush, and said, Moses, Moses. And he said, Here am I.

5 And he said, Draw not nigh hither: put off thy shoes from off thy feet, for the place whereon thou standest is holy ground.

6 Moreover he said, I am the God of thy father, the God of Abraham, the God of Isaac, and the God of Jacob. And Moses hid his face; for he was afraid to look upon God.

7 And the LORD said, I have surely seen the affliction of my people which are in Egypt, and have heard their cry by reason of their taskmasters; for I know their sorrows;

8 And I am come down to deliver them out of the hand of the Egyptians, and to bring them up out of that land unto a good land and a large, unto a land flowing with milk and honey; unto the place of the Canaanites, and the Hittites, and the Amorites, and the Perizzites, and the Hivites, and the Jebusites.

9 Now therefore, behold, the cry of the children of Israel is come unto me: and I have also seen the oppression wherewith the Egyptians oppress them.

10 Come now therefore, and I will send thee unto Pharaoh, that thou mayest bring forth my people the children of Israel out of Egypt.

MEMORY VERSE

Blessed are they that keep judgment, and he that doeth righteousness at all times (Psalm 106:3).

WHAT DOES THE MEMORY VERSE APPLY TO YOUR SPIRITUAL LIFE?

_____

_____

_____

_____

_____

_____

LESSON FOCUS

The Children of Israel were in captivity and waiting for God to bring justice and freedom. God chose Moses as the deliverer of the people from their Egyptian slavery. The lesson focuses on how Moses was sent an unusual invitation from God to learn more about Him and his new assignment.

BIBLE BACKGROUND

Moses was born a Hebrew to his mother Jochebed and his father Amran, both from the tribe of Levi. What should have been a joyous occasion for his parents was met with the realities of society where murder, deceit, sadness, and injustice reigned. The Pharaoh had ordered the midwives to kill the male infants that were born during that time and throw the male newborns into the Nile (Exodus 1:15–22). The midwives Shiphrah and Puah refused to obey the Pharaoh and instead chose to follow God's Word. Moses was born during this tumultuous time. His mother hid him for three months. When Jochebed was no longer able to hide him, she made a papyrus basket that she placed him in on the Nile River. His sister Miriam's assignment was to follow the basket as it floated on the Nile, where one of the princesses of Pharaoh's house was bathing. Miriam encouraged the princess to take the baby from the basket. The princess adopted the baby and she raised him as her own child. The princess named him Moses because she drew him from the water (Exodus 2).

Moses grew up as a prince until one day, he discovered that he was a Hebrew and left the palace. After Moses left the palace, he saw an Egyptian kill a Hebrew, and Moses in turn killed the Egyptian. He thought no one saw him, but some of the slaves did and, fearing for his life, Moses ran to the desert land of Midian. There he met and married Zipporah, the daughter of the priest Jethro. Moses became a shepherd and lived among the Midianites with his wife and their two sons. As Moses was tending to his sheep, he saw something strange happening on Mount Horeb. A bush was burning, but the flames did not engulf the bush and burn it. Moses investigated this miraculous event and then found himself listening and speaking with God. God invites him into the conversation by telling Moses to take off his shoes because he is standing on holy ground (v. 6). God speaks, Moses listens, and then a brief dialogue between the two begins. Moses receives his assignment, then challenges why he is chosen to talk to Pharaoh about freeing the slaves. Moses finally accepts his mission, and a new journey for the Hebrews and the world began.

Exodus reveals God's promise to deliver the Hebrew slaves from bondage in Egypt and their post-slavery journey in the wilderness. As noted by Old Testament scholarship, "...the nation of Israel ... the source of truth and salvation to all the world ... The Israelites had no army, schools, governors, mayors, or temple when they left Egypt. God had to instruct them in their constitutional laws and daily practices. He showed them how to worship and how to have national holidays" (Life Application Bible, 95). The book of Exodus reveals a relationship between God and His people that speaks to His holiness and love. The disobedience, constant complaining, and whining of Israel against the Lord and with one another does not change God's mind to create a new nation. God's tough love comes with a price that the people would pay when they chose not to follow the Lord. Even Moses, God's chosen leader and deliverer of the slaves from Egypt, experienced the consequence for not following God.

SCRIPTURE EXPLORATION
Exodus 3:1–10

The book of Exodus reveals God form-ing a nation from former slaves who were now experiencing freedom and its responsibilities. Chapter 3 provides insight into how their leader Moses was selected by God, Moses' reluctance to serve as a leader, and the process God has already put in place for the Children of Israel when they leave Egypt. The first ten verses of Chapter 3 is the classic story of Moses' invitation from God through a burning bush.

Exodus 3:1
¹ *Now Moses kept the flock of Jethro his father in law, the priest of Midian: and he led the flock to the backside of the desert, and came to the mountain of God, even to Horeb.*

² *And the angel of the LORD appeared unto him in a flame of fire out of the midst of a bush: and he looked, and, behold, the bush burned with fire, and the bush was not consumed.*

In chapter 2, we find that Moses was not named by his Hebrew parents, but by his adopted mother, the princess of the pal-ace. She names him Moses because "she drew him out of the water" (v. 9). Moses grew up in the palace and enjoyed royalty and luxury. His life would be changed and shattered because he killed an Egyptian who had killed one of the slaves. Although Moses thought he had not been noticed, other slaves saw him. Pharaoh was incensed and wanted to kill him. Moses ran for his life to the desert land of Midian. In the desert, he developed a new life and skills that he would later use.

Moses now lives in the desert as a shep-herd for his father-in-law Jethro, who was a priest and had accepted Moses into his family. Moses had grown up in the Egyptian educational system and had to become educated on sheep herding. He no longer lived the life of a privileged nobleman. Moses had to live off the land, tend the flock, and care for people with different beliefs and ways of living.

Moses traveled down the backside of Mount Horeb. Horeb is used interchange-ably with Mount Sinai. According to some biblical scholars, Mount Horeb might mean probably either dry ground, or desolation. Moses was tending sheep and leading them through dry ground to find greener pastures. As a shepherd, Moses' valuable training for sheep would help prepare him for the new life he would soon begin. God used Moses' experiences in the desert to train him for his very challenging task of leading his people. What experiences in your life have pre-pared you for an unexpected event?

Moses saw an unusual event: a bush was burning, but the fire could not consume or engulf it. This fiery bush defied the laws of nature. Moses could not help but to be drawn to it. The bush was probably a bramble or thorn bush. This was God's handcrafted announcement to draw Moses closer. Moses was not afraid of the fire and went to see what was happening. The angel of the Lord appearing as a flame had to be an amazing sight to behold. Additionally, God's presence in the bush is uplifted in Deuteronomy 33:16: "…the favor of him that dwelt in the bush." The divine manifestation of God is expressed throughout the Bible for others to experience, as in Exodus 19:18, 24:17, and Ezekiel 1:27.

God knew how to get Moses' attention!

Exodus 3:3–4
3 *And Moses said, I will now turn aside, and see this great sight, why the bush is not burnt.*

4 *And when the LORD saw that he turned aside to see, God called unto him out of the midst of the bush, and said, Moses, Moses. And he said, Here am I.*

As Moses turned to look at this wondrous sight, God called his name twice. Moses was fascinated by the burning bush that would not burn to the ground. Fire represents God's holiness, and the burning bush was God's holiness displayed for a purpose that Moses would see. God's holiness was seen by the Israelites as the Lord led them by a cloud and smoke on their journey from Egypt (Exodus 13:21). After calling Moses' name, God then directs him to the location where they can meet face to face. God calls Moses' name twice and then says to him, "Here am I" (v. 4). This must have been an amazing experience for Moses—from palace prince to a shepherd, then a personal

encounter with God. Moses walks toward the bush to inspect this phenomenon.

The Bible records other moments where God or His presence is revealed in dramatic or spectacular ways: Abram's vision from God of a "smoking firepot and a blazing torch" (Genesis 15:17); Jacob's dream of the angels ascending and descending on a ladder as the Lord stood above them and spoke to Jacob (Genesis 28:12–13); Balaam's donkey seeing the messenger of God with a sword ready to kill Balaam if he continued traveling on the road with the princes of Moab (Numbers 22:23); and Jesus, after His resurrection, who appears to Mary but is not recognized at first (John 20:15). God continues to appear in our lives in ways that may surprise us, or that we may miss because we are not paying attention or do not understand His presence in our lives.

Exodus 3:5–6
5 *And he said, Draw not nigh hither: put off thy shoes from off thy feet, for the place whereon thou standest is holy ground.*

6 *Moreover he said, I am the God of thy father, the God of Abraham, the God of Isaac, and the God of Jacob. And Moses hid his face; for he was afraid to look upon God.*

God speaks to Moses, and tells him to take off his shoes because he is standing on holy ground (v. 5). First, Moses sees a burning bush, and now he hears God speaking to him—two distinct experiences that would change his life forever. Moses must take off his shoes and stand with his feet on the holy ground. God's holiness mandates that Moses give this particular place utmost reverence. Taking off his shoes, his sandals, represented respect to and humbleness before God. The experience impacts Moses in a very powerful and profound way that he writes about later in the book of Exodus.

This is the first time the Bible uses the word "holy" with reference to God (verse 5). At the burning bush God revealed His holiness in a way it had never been revealed before. Moses was so awed by this experience that later when he wrote his famous victory hymn, he made sure to mention this divine attribute of God's holiness: "Who among the gods is like you, O LORD? Who is like you—majestic in holiness, awesome in glory, working wonders?" (Exodus 15:11). (from http://www.gotquestions.org/burning-bush.html)

Verse 6 highlights the fear and reverence that Moses had for God. God proclaims to Moses that He is the God of Abraham, Isaac, and Jacob. He is the God that his ancestors prayed to, worshiped, and reverenced. Moses immediately acknowledges God's holiness and refuses to even peek at this amazing God. The word for fear in Hebrew is *yirah*. Mike Bennett says that fear "usually refers to the fear of God as viewed in a positive quality. This fear acknowledges God's good intentions (Exodus 20:20). This fear is produced by God's Word (Psalm 119:38; Proverbs 2:5)

and makes a person receptive to wisdom and knowledge (Proverbs 1:7, 9:10)" (Bennett, 470–471).

Giving honor and reverence to God is what believers should do. God is the only true God and deserves respect and honor from all. The Bible often refers to fearing God as part of worship (e.g., 1 Samuel 12:24; Proverbs 16:6; Hebrews 12:28). Like Moses, we too should honor God quickly and without hesitation in our worship, our everyday lives, and in those times when we have the opportunity to give more. We might be quiet, bold, or unsung heroes, but we can all do something that makes a difference and has a positive impact in the lives of others. Our relationship with Christ provides us with the strength and wisdom to go beyond our comfort zone. We are expected to do more because the Holy Spirit's transforming power and Christ inside us will lead us to our burning bush experiences and know the voice of God. Our obedience to God is greater than our sacrifice.

God appealed to Moses' curiosity through the burning bush and entreated him to learn more of why the bush was not completely burning. The Lord's presence was confirmed through the angel that spoke to Moses. God began a relationship with Moses that he accepted and took seriously. We too must respect and obey God's Words in our lives as we serve the only true and living God.

Exodus 3:7–10

7 *And the LORD said, I have surely seen*

the affliction of my people which are in Egypt, and have heard their cry by reason of their taskmasters; for I know their sorrows;

8 *And I am come down to deliver them out of the hand of the Egyptians, and to bring them up out of that land unto a good land and a large, unto a land flowing with milk and honey; unto the place of the Canaanites, and the Hittites, and the Amorites, and the Perizzites, and the Hivites, and the Jebusites.*

9 *Now therefore, behold, the cry of the children of Israel is come unto me: and I have also seen the oppression wherewith the Egyptians oppress them.*

10 *Come now therefore, and I will send thee unto Pharaoh, that thou mayest bring forth my people the children of Israel out of Egypt.*

After God invites Moses to witness the burning bush, Moses refused to look at God because of his respect and reverence for God. The Lord proceeded to explain the reasons for Moses having to meet Him in such a unique and miraculous experience. Moses is given an invitational directive by the Lord to fulfill His promise to deliver the slaves to freedom. Moses had to face plenty of drama and intrigue in his life: Pharaoh's proclamation of death to any male Hebrew infant; his papyrus baby basket set in the Nile by his mother and carefully watched by his sister; Miriam encouraging the Egyptian princess to adopt the baby boy;

and finally being raised and educated as an Egyptian prince. Moses' life drama continues with his killing an Egyptian in defense of a slave, only to be caught and singled out for his terrible act by other Hebrews; he then ran for his life into the land of Midian.

Despite the life-threatening events, God had a plan for Moses that would not be stopped by Pharaoh's violent leadership or Moses' own impetuous actions. Moses returned to Egypt as God had requested of him with his wife Zipporah, their two sons, and the blessing of his father-in-law Jethro (Exodus 2:11–15, 4:18–20). Moses was the deliverer that would set the captives free as God had promised (Genesis 15:16, 46:3, 4).

For 40 years, Moses lived in Midian with his new family. He would spend another 40 years wandering in the desert with the other disobedient Israelites (Numbers 15:1–21:35). The number 40 is a significant number in the Bible. Joshua, Caleb, and the other spies searched the Promised Land for 40 days (Numbers 13:25). For 40 days, the flood waters moved to cover the earth as Noah, his family, and the animals on the ark waited for God's deliverance from the flood (Genesis 7:17). Jesus was in the wilderness and tempted by Satan for 40 days (Matthew 4:1–11; Mark 1:12–13; Luke 4:1–13).

Although Moses was humbled by the presence of God, verse 11 explains how he was not comfortable with God's request for him to be the deliverer. Moses was not ready to leave and become a leader, the hero, to deliver the Hebrew slaves to freedom. Eventually, Moses accepted God's leadership role and plans after God strongly told him that his brother Aaron would assist. The journey was difficult and very challenging, but Moses and the Hebrew people survived the plagues and Pharaoh's harshness. Moses delivered the people from Egypt as God had instructed. Although their journey from Egypt was difficult, God delivered them to a new place—the Promised Land. Although Moses was not able to enter into the Promised Land because of his disobedience, God did allow him to see where His people and future generations would live if they obeyed the Lord (Deuteronomy 34:1–4).

PRACTICAL APPLICATION

PERSONAL APPLICATION

1. Write a blog post or email close friends about how God is present in your life in expected and unexpected ways. Share how God's presence is a blessing to you and how this knowledge impacts how you interact with others.

2. List three events that reminded you of God's holiness and how humbled you are before God. How did this deepen your faith? Once a week, write a word or two that describes God's holiness, and how you are humbled in knowing Him through Jesus Christ. Keep a diary or journal of your words. Design

a creative art piece, such as a collage or wall hanging, using your words. Share your reflections with others and meditate on God's holiness.

COMMUNITY APPLICATION

1. Partner with others and develop a sacred place where people can come together to pray and discuss justice and how they can make a difference. Plan how and when the actions for justice will happen and who will be involved.

2. Create a community garden with fruits, vegetables, and a variety of plants. Provide food for those in the community who need to eat. Work with other ministries or community groups to cook and serve the food to those who do not have enough to eat.

MEDITATION

Lord, like Moses, we need to take off our shoes and stand humbled before You. Taking off our shoes is a blessing because we have shoes to wear. So many people in this world have no shoes and suffer the consequences of greed, selfishness, and injustice. Unlike Moses, they do not have someone to care for them or advocate for their needs. Sometimes Lord, we need someone to stand up for us. Taking off our shoes is submission before You. We are reminded that You are in charge and deserve all the praise, glory, and honor. Your presence is powerful and transforming. Each day, we should bless You and thank You for allowing us to stand in Your presence and know that You are our wonderful God. Thank You for allowing us to worship You and share Your goodness and justice with others.

PRAYER

Dear Lord, we live in an unjust world. Show me how to fight for those whose voices are silent and whose lives are considered meaningless. Hear, O Lord, the empty hearts of those whose lives look full of joy and life, but are hurting on the inside. Lord, we seek Your face, and want to walk humbling before You with Christ, yet we do not always choose to follow Your Word. Give us another chance and create a new Spirit within us. We thank You and we praise You. Amen.

BIBLIOGRAPHY

Baker, Warren, and Eugene Carpenter. *The Complete Word Study Dictionary: Old Testament.* Chattanooga, TN: AMG Publishers, 2003. 470-471.

Bennett, Mike. Fear of the Lord: What Does It Mean? www.openbible.info/topics/fear_of_the_lord. Accessed July 27, 2014.

http://biblehub.com/commentaries/cambridge/exodus/3.htm. Accessed July 27, 2014.

"Why did God speak to Moses out of the burning bush?" http://www.gotquestions.org/burning-bush.html. Accessed July 27, 2014.

Life Application Study Bible, NIV. Wheaton, Illinois and Grand Rapids, Michigan, Tyndale House Publishers, Inc. and Zondervan Publishing House, 1997. 96-101.

The Significance of the Number 40. www.ecclesia.org/truth/40.htm. Accessed August 9, 2014.

NOTES

CHAPTER 5

SEEKING SALVATION AND CHOOSING COMPASSION

SCRIPTURE LESSON

Luke 10:25–37

BACKGROUND SCRIPTURES

Leviticus 19:18; Deuteronomy 6:5; Matthew 19:16–22;
Mark 10:17–22; Luke 10; John 4:1–42

QUESTION

When you find yourself in a difficult situation, who or what do you turn to for help? Why? Is this your usual first response? Explain.

AN UNEXPECTED BLESSING

A terrible tornado had blown through the small community. Homes were destroyed and lives were changed forever. The Turner family—David, Daniella, and their three children—had moved to a picturesque and quiet community only a month ago. Now, their dreams were crushed, and hopelessness had set in. The tornado had moved with such force that their home had been picked up and tossed like a dollhouse miles away. All of them were safe, but rebuilding was such a daunting task. They thanked the Lord for their safety, but could not help but ask why. Further, the community officials had said that everyone needed to leave the area until it was safe to return. What would happen and where would they go?

A neighbor, Mrs. Brown, had been quite fortunate. Her home was the only house left standing on the block. She was praising God as she walked to see what she could do to help others. She stopped to talk with David, Daniella, and their children. She knew they had a newborn and wanted to make sure they were okay. Mrs. Brown immediately hugged them and offered to give them a ride to her cousins in the city so they could be safe. David and Daniella could not believe she was offering such help. After discussing the opportunity for a moment, they decided to take Mrs. Brown up on her offer until they could figure out what to do next. What a blessing! Mrs. Brown's cousin had a five-bedroom house and dog. There was more than enough room. The children could play in the yard, help care for the pet, and make new friends. It would take some time, but everyone knew that things would work out.

That night, the Turner family prayed, thanked God for such a wonderful opportunity, and asked Him to forgive them for not leaning on Him in their time of despair.

DISCUSSION

When we find ourselves in stressful situations, what thoughts run through our minds? Do we blame God, joke, cry, pray? Share how you typically respond to stress and the results of your initial reaction. What coping mechanisms do you think Christians should depend on?

TRANSITION

Our Scripture text is one of the more familiar passages in the Bible, the parable of the Good Samaritan. This lesson highlights salvation, loving God and our neighbor, and having an attitude of love in action that reflects how people should live their lives in relationship to one another. Jesus' emphasis on compassion and love are still expected of us today.

SCRIPTURE VOCABULARY

Samaritan—A person who lived in Samaria or in the area known today as Nablus. Samaritans practice Judaism in a particular form based on their understandings and writings of their version of the Pentateuch. Jews and Samaritans did not get along because of how they believed, understood, and practiced the Law of Moses.

Samaria—Built by Omri, a king of Israel, around 920 B.C., Samaria was located near Palestine and Shechem. The city of Samaria was named after the former owner and was known for its exquisitely ornate buildings. Refer to 1 Kings 22:39, 1 Kings 16:32–33, and 2 Kings 10:18–28 for additional information.

"The Jericho Road"—A contemporary term used to describe the 17-mile journey from Jerusalem to Jericho and vice versa. The road is known as the "Way of Blood" because many people were injured, robbed, and killed as they traveled on this road.

Priest—The descendants of Aaron from the tribe of Levi. The responsibilities and duties of the priests were to offer the daily sacrifices, represent the people before the Lord, and serve as counselors to the people on how to live and follow God's ways and caretakers of the tabernacle (Life Application, 136).

Levite—Workers of the temple who did not have as many responsibilities as the priests, and served in the various cities where Jewish people lived. Unlike the priests, they did not serve for life.

SCRIPTURE REFERENCE

Luke 10:25–37

25 And, behold, a certain lawyer stood up, and tempted him, saying, Master, what shall I do to inherit eternal life?

26 He said unto him, What is written in the law? how readest thou?

27 And he answering said, Thou shalt love the Lord thy God with all thy heart, and with all thy soul, and with all thy strength, and with all thy mind; and thy neighbour as thyself.

28 And he said unto him, Thou hast answered right: this do, and thou shalt live.

29 But he, willing to justify himself, said unto Jesus, And who is my neighbour?

30 And Jesus answering said, A certain man went down from Jerusalem to Jericho, and fell among thieves, which stripped him of his raiment, and wounded him, and departed, leaving him half dead.

31 And by chance there came down a certain priest that way: and when he saw him, he passed by on the other side.

32 And likewise a Levite, when he was at the place, came and looked on him, and passed by on the other side.

33 But a certain Samaritan, as he journeyed, came where he was: and when he saw him, he had compassion on him,

34 And went to him, and bound up his wounds, pouring in oil and wine, and set him on his own beast, and brought him to an inn, and took care of him.

35 And on the morrow when he departed, he took out two pence, and gave them to the host, and said unto him, Take care of him; and whatsoever thou spendest more, when I come again, I will repay thee.

36 Which now of these three, thinkest thou, was neighbour unto him that fell among the thieves?

37 And he said, He that shewed mercy on him. Then said Jesus unto him, Go, and do thou likewise.

MEMORY VERSE

Neither is there salvation in any other: for there is none other name under heaven given among men, whereby we must be saved (Acts 2:4–12).

HOW DOES THE MEMORY VERSE APPLY TO YOUR SPIRITUAL LIFE?

_____

_____

_____

_____

_____

_____

LESSON FOCUS

The focus of this lesson has two parts: 1) Jesus is our salvation who shows us that compassion and love are required of us, even when we would rather not. 2) Loving others requires us to go beyond our safe limitations.

BIBLE BACKGROUND

The Gospel of Luke was written in about 90 A.D. in Rome or Caesarea, and is credited to a non-Hebrew writer, Luke. He was a very educated man—a Greek physician—who had an excellent command of the Greek language and knowledge of the various cultures and religious environments during that time. Luke has the distinction of probably being the only known Gentile writer of the New Testament. He is the author of Acts of the Apostles, which was written for Theophilus and Gentiles to read. However, Jews, Gentiles, and those who want to have a deeper understanding of Jesus as the Messiah, His ministry, and His message will appreciate Luke's attention to detail, his use of eyewitness accounts to support Jesus' work, and the compassion and love that Jesus gave to those who were outcast and poor in society.

Luke provides the reader with an opportunity in his 24 chapters to experience Jesus' miracle birth, its impact on the community, and the heavenly response. Luke notes the theological debates and discussions that Jesus had the age of 12 in the temple with the religious officials (2:41–52). Luke also presents Jesus' connection with John, the one who prepared the way for and baptized Jesus (3:1–22). From Jesus' baptism to His genealogy to His temptation in the wilderness, Luke reveals the human and divine side of Jesus (3:23–4:13). Jesus' understanding of the pain and frustrations of others is real, because He experienced the sharp twists and turns of life too.

Luke details the ministry of Jesus in the regions of Galilee (4:14–9:50), both Judea and Perea (9:51–19:27), and Jerusalem (19:28–24:53). During Jesus' times of ministry, he selected his 12 disciples, healed people who were blind or sick, and gave hope to those who were unable to help themselves. Luke records Jesus' prayer life and the power of prayer, hymns of celebrations, 23 parables of Jesus, 20 miracles, and several of His discourses that challenge government and religious officials. His Gospels also declares Jesus as the Messiah, and demonstrates the power of love and compassion for others. The Gospel writer chooses to highlight the importance of women in the life and ministry of Jesus from birth to death to His resurrection. He also provides the reader with an opportunity to see Jesus caring for children as a reminder that they are precious to God.

Luke keeps Jesus' ministry and walk focused on Him as the Messiah, who was sent from God from birth to His death on the Cross in Jerusalem. Jesus' resurrection is the fulfillment of God's promise from the Old Testament. After His resurrection, Jesus does not leave His disciples alone. The Holy Spirit, as Jesus promised, would come to provide comfort and guidance. The New Covenant through Christ is alive and for all to experience and believe.

SCRIPTURE EXPLORATION

Luke 10 begins with Jesus selecting 70 disciples and commissioning them to go out and heal, preach, teach, and tell others the Good News of salvation (vv. 1–12). In addition to the twelve disciples Jesus had already chosen, He now selects another group to address the people's needs and speak about Christ. Jesus sent the commissioned disciples out in pairs across the land. The selection of the 70 is the same number Moses selected during their wilderness journey to assist with the people's needs (Exodus 18:19,

24:1–9). Jesus states that the 70 are to receive compensation for their needs, and should not stay any place that they are not wanted (v. 10).

The Scripture lesson, Luke 10:25–37, is divided into two parts—salvation and loving others. First, a scribe (a lawyer) challenges Jesus. Scribes were experts in the Law because of their knowledge and responsibility to teach the Scriptures. They had no authority, but used their connections with people in authority to assume a role of superiority and justify themselves. Secondly, Jesus tells the parable of the Good Samaritan in response to the scribe's question about neighbors, being neighborly, and showing compassion.

Luke 10:25–26

25 *And, behold, a certain lawyer stood up, and tempted him, saying, Master, what shall I do to inherit eternal life?*

26 *He said unto him, What is written in the law? how readest thou?*

Our popular parable for this lesson, the Good Samaritan, is an example of Jesus' interaction with an expert in the Law, who wanted to catch Him misspeaking words of judgment against God's Laws. However, his test of Jesus could not ensnare or provoke Him to speak or act contrary to God's Word.

In verse 25, the scribe asks Jesus how to "inherit eternal life." According to Keener, the word "life meant long life on the land, but many latter Jewish interpreters read it as a promise to eternal life. Jesus applies the principle to eternal life as well..." (1993, 218). The lawyer already knew the answer. The question is asked again in Luke 18:18–19 by a chief ruler. Scholars note that this was a question that was often asked (Mark 10:17, Matthew 25:46, Luke 18:26–27). Variations on the question of eternal life are found throughout the Gospels from "entering the kingdom of heaven" to "being saved." John's Gospel includes the term "eternal life" more frequently than the Synoptic Gospels (NIV Study Bible, 1467).

Jesus took an unconventional approach that sometimes confused people or challenged their beliefs. An example of this is found in Matthew 19:16–23 in the case of the rich young man. The young man knew the Law, but he did not want to wholeheartedly live it out by giving up his possessions. Even the twelve disciples who followed Jesus were not clear on who would be saved (Matthew 19:25–28). Jesus answers the lawyer's question with two questions in verse 26: "What is written in the law? how readest thou?" Answering a question with a question is not always the most direct response, yet Jesus uses this technique over 25 times throughout the Gospels (Matthew 21:16, Mark 7:17–18, John 11:8).

The first few verses of our Scripture lesson are about salvation, but Jesus' responses are not limited to a simple answer. Salvation is God's "gracious provision through faith of the One who would remove sin" (chosenpeople.com, July 6, 2014). It is through the sacrificing of animals and their blood in the Old Testament and the life, death (shedding of blood), and resurrection of Christ in the New Testament. In fact, the question is not about what is salvation, but about how to respond to God's love to inherit eternal life. The scribe does not realize that his questions provide Jesus an opportunity to expand upon the standard answer to this question. God's love and our response will be unpacked for the lawyer, as well as future generations. The lawyer's question and Jesus' questions and responses are questions that we too must answer.

Luke 10:27–29

27 And he answering said, Thou shalt love the Lord thy God with all thy heart, and with all thy soul, and with all thy strength, and with all thy mind; and thy neighbour as thyself.

28 And he said unto him, Thou hast answered right: this do, and thou shalt live.

29 But he, willing to justify himself, said unto Jesus, And who is my neighbour?

The lawyer does not challenge why Jesus answered the question with questions, maybe because he was confident in his own answers. The lawyer's responses about love and neighborliness were correct, and are recorded in the Old Testament (Deuteronomy 6:5, Leviticus 19:8).

The lawyer knew that loving God with all his heart, strength, and mind were of utmost importance and chose to live this out in his own way. The lawyer limited his answer to his worldview and religious understanding. Like some of us, he needed to step outside his parochial perspective to think beyond his narrow worldview.

Jesus understood that the lawyer's love was selective and not encompassing non-Jews. Jesus agrees with the scribe's responses and tells him, do what the Law commands about love and he will have eternal life (vv. 28–29). Although the scribe knew the answer to the first question, he asks another question he thought would require more from Jesus and validate himself (v. 29). This allowed Jesus to challenge the lawyer's beliefs further; He then answers the expert's question by telling the parable of the Good Samaritan.

Luke 10:30
30 *And Jesus answering said, A certain man went down from Jerusalem to Jericho, and fell among thieves, which stripped him of his raiment, and wounded him, and departed, leaving him half dead.*

Traveling from Jerusalem to Jericho is about 17 miles. The road to Jericho was known as the "Way of Blood" because this treacherous path was infamous for murder, robberies, beatings, and other horrific injuries that occurred. This parable's listeners would be unsurprised that someone was beaten, robbed, and left to die by thieves on this road.

Anyone who traveled on this road was subject to harm and danger because of its landscape. The road was rocky and stretched across the desert. This provided hiding places for bandits. Although people traveled on this road, the timing of travelers, the desert heat, and the area's dryness restricted injured people from crawling or walking to safety. Each traveler would have an altitude shift of 3,300 feet, between Jerusalem at 2,500 feet above sea level to Jericho 800 feet below sea level.

Jesus does not name the traveler, nor identify his religious beliefs or anything else about him—the hearer only knows he was a traveler. Therefore, the hearer only knows that here is a man in need, and his religious beliefs, homeland, and family background are not held against him.

Luke 10:31–35
31 *And by chance there came down a certain priest that way: and when he saw him, he passed by on the other side.*

32 *And likewise a Levite, when he was at the place, came and looked on him, and passed by on the other side.*

33 *But a certain Samaritan, as he journeyed, came where he was: and when he saw him, he had compassion on him,*

34 *And went to him, and bound up his wounds, pouring in oil and wine, and set him on his own beast, and brought him to an inn, and took care of him.*

35 *And on the morrow when he departed, he took out two pence, and gave them to the host, and said unto him, Take care of*

him; and whatsoever thou spendest more, when I come again, I will repay thee.

The unknown man was badly hurt—at risk of death—and waited for someone to help him. Jesus stated how three different people had the chance to help him. The priest was the first to see the injured man. Jesus tells His audience that the priest was on the same side of the road as the victim, but chose not to help. Instead, he crossed to the other side of the road, giving no words of comfort. God's servant intentionally chose to ignore the needs of someone else.

Next, Jesus states that the second person was a Levite. Like the priest, he is on his way to Jericho from Jerusalem. Seeing the beaten man, the Levite also decided not to help, passing by on the other side. Jesus gives no reason that the Levite or priest didn't help. Maybe they felt they wouldn't be able to carry him to safety. Maybe they did not feel like taking the time to help because they were too busy thinking about their plans in Jericho with their families and friends.

Some suggest the priest or the Levite had ceremonial duties and would be defiled if they touched the man. It was unlawful for either of them to touch something or someone that was bleeding or had been hurt or dead if they were on their way to the temple for any religious or ceremonial activities. As Keener states, "Priests were supposed to avoid especially impurity from a corpse; Pharisees thought one would contact it if even one's shadow touched the corpse" (218). Remember, however, they left Jerusalem—where the temple was located—and traveled to Jericho. Therefore, there were no religious or urgent matters requiring haste. Both men chose not to touch the beaten man or come too close to him. Since the man looked dead, they decided to follow one set of religious rules, but not the rule of mercy. As noted by Keener, "…rules were rules; although the rule of mercy would take precedence if the man were clearly alive, the man looked as if he might be dead (v. 30), and the priest did not wish to take a chance" (218).

Both men were Jewish and knew that loving God required loving neighbors as themselves. Each man chose not to exercise love or compassion. They walked away and left the man broken, bruised, and battered. Would someone care for him or leave him to die a lonely and painful death? Have you ignored people who obviously needed help? Why?

The third person to come along was the Samaritan man. It is interesting that Jesus would suggest a Samaritan as a character in the parable since Jews and Samaritans did not get along. Unlike the priest and the Levite, the Samaritan takes the time to care for the hurt man by bandaging his wounds, allowing the man to ride on the animal while he walked, and taking him to the inn, where he will be cared for while he healed (vv. 34–35). Both men were strangers, but the Samaritan was willing to show love and compassion by assisting another person in need.

Jesus purposely chose the Samaritan as the hero of the story to challenge the cultural and religious beliefs of his story's Jewish listeners. This is not the only time that Jesus intentionally includes a Samaritan; in the Gospel of John, Jesus interacts with a Samaritan woman (John 4:1–42). Jesus initiates a full conversation with the Samaritan woman during the middle of the day at Jacob's well. He clearly violated the religious and social taboos of his day—Jews and Samaritans do not worship together, meet, talk, or socialize for any reason—and had no right to speak with her since she was a woman alone in public. However, Jesus continued to establish a new order for living with one another. Both groups, Jews and Samaritans, and those who do not get along with one another today, have the opportunity to seek and accept the salvation of Jesus Christ in their lives, and choose to coexist compassionately. Consequently, the despised Samaritan woman becomes a mighty witness to Christ's power and salvation to transform lives.

Luke 10:36–37

36 *Which now of these three, thinkest thou, was neighbour unto him that fell among the thieves?*

37 *And he said, He that shewed mercy on him. Then said Jesus unto him, Go, and do thou likewise.*

Jesus chose to tell Jewish people a parable that includes two Jews and a Samaritan, since the Jews and Samaritans hated each other. The Jews, who thought of themselves "as pure descendants of Abraham, despised the Samaritans because they were descendants of the mixed marriages between Jews and non-Jews in the northern kingdom" (Life Application Bible, 1695). Therefore, by highlighting the actions of the priest, the Levite, and the Samaritan, Jesus adds an unexpected twist for the scribe and other listeners. After sharing the parable, Jesus asked the lawyer, "Which now of these three, thinkest thou, was neighbour unto him that fell among the thieves?" (v. 36). The lawyer knew the answer to this question too; there was no wiggle room for him to deny that the Samaritan was the good neighbor. Although the lawyer does acknowledge the one "who showed mercy on the injured man" (v. 37), he could not even say "the Samaritan." The animosity between the Jews and Samaritans was too ingrained for him to overcome. There are many people, including Christians, who are like this in many areas of their lives.

DISCUSSION

1. Read Deuteronomy 6:5 and Leviticus 19:18. How do these Scriptures apply to loving ourselves first and then others? Describe how you love yourself and others as defined by God. Do you struggle with loving yourself but not loving others in tangible ways?

2. Give possibilities why the lawyer could not say the word "Samaritan" when he answered Jesus' question (v. 35).

3. Read about Jesus' visit to Martha and Mary (vv. 38–41). How does this relate to the themes found in the Scripture lesson text of the Good Samaritan? Are the themes similar or different?

PRACTICAL APPLICATION

PERSONAL APPLICATION

1. Keep a journal of how God has blessed you, and your responses. Maintain your journal with words, images, or other ways that help you to express your relationship with Christ. Every week, review and read your journal. Note how many times you helped others who were in need and how others helped you.

2. How can you change your responses when others are in need? How can you work with others to impact a community in crisis? Look online for various resources that may assist you in showing compassion for others.

COMMUNITY APPLICATION

1. Violence comes in many forms and is very prevalent in our communities and around the world. Work with community groups to plan opportunities to address issues of violence. Organize or assist with providing workshops, victim assistance programs, and job programs for ex-offenders, teens, unemployed, and others.

2. Volunteer with your church's social justice ministry or benevolent ministry and coordinate possibilities to assist church members who need assistance.

MEDITATION

Sometimes we are right about whatever the topic, idea, or action is, but also limited in our knowledge or understanding. For instance, it is true that honey is sweet, but it can also cause sickness or death for some. In learning and applying God's Word in our lives, we must endeavor to dig deeper and apply the Word in our lives regardless of the circumstances. How we apply God's Word in our relationship with others requires us to go a little deeper and trust God more. As we allow the Holy Spirit to guide us, let us be mindful to want and need God's love in our lives. Each moment and every second of the day is a taste of God's goodness and love toward us. Meditate on the love of Christ and allow the joy of Jesus' love to dwell in us. We are blessed to know and experience that the love of Jesus is for today and always.

PRAYER

Lord, thank You for loving us and caring for us even when we do not always love others. Show us how to love others because You first loved us. Jesus, we bless You and magnify You. Open our eyes when they are shut to see and do what You would have us to do daily. Thank You Lord. Amen.

BIBLIOGRAPHY

biblehub.com/topical/s/samaria.htm. ATS Bible Dictionary. Accessed June 25, 2014.

biblestudytools.com/dictionary/samaritans/. Accessed June 25, 2014.

www.bible.ca. Accessed June 25 and 29, 2014.

www.gci.org/bible/luke/goodsam. Accessed July 9, 2014.

mondaymorningreview.wordpress.com. Accessed July 5, 2014.

Keener, Craig. *The IVP Bible Background Commentary*. Downers Grove, Illinois: IntervVarsity Press, 1993. 217-218.

Life Application Study Bible, NIV. Wheaton, Illinois and Grand Rapids, Michigan: Tyndale House Publishers, Inc. and Zondervan Publishing House, 1997. 1655, 1656, 1693-1696.

New International Version - Study Bible. Grand Rapids, Michigan: Zondervan Publishing House, 1984. 1558.

NOTES

_____

_____

_____

_____

_____

_____

WORSHIP ANCHORS MY SOUL

SCRIPTURE LESSON
John 4:7–24

BACKGROUND SCRIPTURES
Genesis 33:19, 48:22; 2 Kings 17; Jeremiah 2:13; Mark 5:29; Revelation 7:17

QUESTION
As a child of God, how do we reflect love or thankfulness for Him despite the spiritual wickedness of our times? How can you describe the emotions, passion, energy, and feelings of recognizing God's sovereignty over our lives? Explain.

MY HEART BELONGS TO YOU

During a high school baseball game, one of the players became deathly ill, suddenly falling to the ground without any warning. Most spectators thought he fainted because of the humidity and heat, hoping he would get to his feet quickly, but this was not the case. He did not move. Someone called an ambulance, which rushed the young man to the hospital. A doctor examined the young man and found he had an enlarged heart expanding faster than his physical growth, which would eventually lead to his early death unless he received a new heart.

Besides needing a heart donor, the parents' other pressing concern was the cost of medical care. The cost for the surgical procedure and hospitalization was too much for them to pay. Their insurance coverage was inadequate. Their bank accounts were already exhausted. The parents began selling all their assets—including furniture, clothing, and cars—to pay for the son's expenses. Every available resource was liquidated, and it was still not enough! His father felt he would do anything to save his son. Finally, tears rolling down his cheeks, he decided to give his own heart to his son. He sacrificed himself for his son, giving his all because of his devotion. He poured out his heart because of his love for his only son. The young man lived and spent the rest of his life remembering and honoring his father's sacrifice.

Are we willing to give all to God? The father is willing to give his heart to his son. Can you give your heart in godly worship? Worship is anchored by a Spirit-filled worshiper expressing deep and abiding love to God. Worship is giving all that we have to God, even to the point of being willing to sacrifice ourselves. We are expected to give our all, all that we have, all that we are, every ounce of energy that we can muster in our worship of God. God loves His only Son, and we ought to love Jesus so much so that we give all to worship Him.

DISCUSSION
Have you ever wanted to give up because you believed that you had no way out, but God made a way for you to make it through? Explain.

TRANSITION
Jesus' teaching causes us to reflect on our lifestyle as a community of believers. This lesson's Scripture is a refreshing story about a woman and her relationship to God. She lives in a community without a full knowledge of God or godliness. Our lesson focuses on the importance of worship and how people encounter Jesus in their daily activities.

SCRIPTURE VOCABULARY
Samaritan—A person who lived in Samaria or in the area known today as Nablus. Samaritans follow or practice Judaism in a particular form based on their understandings and writings of their version of the Pentateuch. Jews and Samaritans did not get along because of how they believed, understood, and practiced the Law of Moses.

Worship—A pervasive attitude of reverence, adoration, and actions expressed toward God. Worship suggests revering God through a humble posture while also serving Him in daily activities. Although the form of worship may change, what remains constant is one's sincerity and authenticity within the heart. Listening to the Word of God, sacrificial offerings, and prayers represent the essence of worship.

Sychar—A city of Samaria described as a place of untruth or falsehood, likely because Samaritans were though to have an incomplete understanding of God and their antagonistic relationship with the Jews. Geographically, Sychar is considered to be in close proximity to Shechem or Askar, depending on the exact location of Jacob's well, which was still active during the time of Jesus (Actemier, 1985).

SCRIPTURE REFERENCE

John 4:7–24
7 There cometh a woman of Samaria to draw water: Jesus saith unto her, Give me to drink.

8 (For his disciples were gone away unto the city to buy meat.)

9 Then saith the woman of Samaria unto him, How is it that thou, being a Jew, askest drink of me, which am a woman of Samaria? for the Jews have no dealings with the Samaritans.

10 Jesus answered and said unto her, If thou knewest the gift of God, and who it is that saith to thee, Give me to drink; thou wouldest have asked of him, and he would have given thee living water.

11 The woman saith unto him, Sir, thou hast nothing to draw with, and the well is deep: from whence then hast thou that living water?

12 Art thou greater than our father Jacob, which gave us the well, and drank thereof himself, and his children, and his cattle?

13 Jesus answered and said unto her, Whosoever drinketh of this water shall thirst again:

14 But whosoever drinketh of the water that I shall give him shall never thirst; but the water that I shall give him shall be in him a well of water springing up into everlasting life.

15 The woman saith unto him, Sir, give me this water, that I thirst not, neither come hither to draw.

16 Jesus saith unto her, Go, call thy husband, and come hither.

17 The woman answered and said, I have no husband. Jesus said unto her, Thou hast well said, I have no husband:

18 For thou hast had five husbands; and he whom thou now hast is not thy husband: in that saidst thou truly.

19 The woman saith unto him, Sir, I perceive that thou art a prophet.

20 Our fathers worshipped in this mountain; and ye say, that in Jerusalem is the place where men ought to worship.

21 Jesus saith unto her, Woman, believe me, the hour cometh, when ye shall neither in this mountain, nor yet at Jerusalem, worship the Father.

22 Ye worship ye know not what: we know what we worship: for salvation is of the Jews.

23 But the hour cometh, and now is, when the true worshippers shall worship the Father in spirit and in truth: for the Father seeketh such to worship him.

24 God is a Spirit: and they that worship him must worship him in spirit and in truth.

MEMORY VERSE

God is a Spirit: and they that worship him must worship him in spirit and in truth (John 4:24).

HOW DOES THE MEMORY VERSE APPLY TO YOUR SPIRITUAL LIFE?

_____

_____

_____

_____

_____

_____

_____

LESSON FOCUS

Worship, both private and public, is an expression of our complete and unconditional devotion to Jesus, and it is a matter of the heart. Jesus is the subject and objective of our worship and is expressed far beyond simple intellectual comprehension. Geography, gender, or social standing are not important when it comes to worshiping Jesus. Whether you are alone or in a group, God must be our hero. In every condition and under every situation, God has kept us. Wherever you are is the place to worship God. His divine power allows us to sincerely express ourselves in worship.

BIBLE BACKGROUND

The location of the story was Sychar, which is modern Askar, near the ancient city of Shechem. According to tradition, Jacob built a well there that was still in active use in Jesus' time. The text follows a conversation between Jesus and a Samaritan woman. Samaritans are the offspring of Jews and Assyrians, and had an antagonistic relationship with the Jews for two reasons. One, Samaritans worshiped on the mountain in Gerizim, not Jerusalem. Secondly, the primarily Jewish population in the Southern Kingdom felt superior to their more ethnically mixed counterparts in the North. This longstanding disagreement was still relevant in Jesus' time. The Samaritan woman meets Jesus as He is travelling from Judea to Galilee. He takes a shorter route and goes through Samaria, in spite of the animosity between the Jews and the Samaritans. He is tired and weary from His journey, so He requests a drink. The conversation quickly moves from the physical water to spiritual water. The woman is hesitant because she does not realize Jesus' divine nature or the meaning of living water. She recognizes Jesus as a prophet, but not yet as the Messiah.

SCRIPTURE EXPLORATION
John 4:7–24

In our Scripture text, a woman goes to a well seeking to draw water. She encounters Jesus, who changes her life. This transformative encounter is different because she faces truths expressed in an unfamiliar way. She is challenged to recognize her own failures in her earthly and spiritual relationships, which have been devastating. Her spirituality is incomplete, she has been involved in five failed marriages, and it appears that she is living with a man without being married. This Samaritan woman finds herself in a spiritual quagmire because she doesn't understand God's plan. Her faith in God is based on her location, not dedication to the invisible God of Abraham, Isaac, and Jacob. The historic difference between Samaritans and Jews impedes her ability to properly see God in bringing Jesus to her. In the heat of the day, she recognizes the one Man not only interested in her life, but her lifestyle after she acknowledges Jesus as a prophet. She comes to this old well that Jacob built and finds fresh water to quench a thirst that is not earthly, but spiritual.

John 4:7–9

7 *There cometh a woman of Samaria to draw water: Jesus saith unto her, Give me to drink.*

8 *(For his disciples were gone away unto the city to buy meat.)*

9 *Then saith the woman of Samaria unto him, How is it that thou, being a Jew, askest drink of me, which am a woman of Samaria? for the Jews have no dealings with the Samaritans.*

Jesus traveled from Judea back to Galilee after learning how the Pharisees were complaining about His popularity (John 4:1–2). They wanted to harm him because the people were listening and paying more attention to Jesus than the Pharisees. Jesus left Judea because it was not His time to die. While traveling, He grew tired and decided to rest at a well—Jacob's well in Samaria. Although Samaria was a place that Jews avoided, Jesus, a Jew, purposely travels there. As Jesus rests, a Samaritan woman comes to the well. Jesus' meaningful conversation with her would change her life forever.

Women often came to the well not alone but in groups, either early or later to stay out of the sun. However, this woman comes at noon, suggesting she was isolated and an outcast in her community. Perhaps she felt the weight of shame as a result of her lifestyle (MacArthur, 2006, 1550). A well was also a place where women came to meet and socialize.

The disciples had gone ahead into the city to purchase food from the Samaritans. This is significant because it shows their willingness to buy from a community that more rigid-thinking or conservative minded Jews would find to be unthinkable (MacArthur, 1550).

The Hebrews had strict social regulations for men and women. It was socially taboo for a man to speak with a woman alone, and even more damaging for a rabbi to speak to a woman in public alone. In the case here, this taboo was compounded by the long-standing animosity between Samaritans and Jews (MacArthur, 1550).

John 4:10–12

10 *Jesus answered and said unto her, If thou knewest the gift of God, and who it is*

that saith to thee, Give me to drink; thou wouldest have asked of him, and he would have given thee living water.

¹¹ *The woman saith unto him, Sir, thou hast nothing to draw with, and the well is deep: from whence then hast thou that living water?*

¹² *Art thou greater than our father Jacob, which gave us the well, and drank thereof himself, and his children, and his cattle?*

Jesus responds to the woman's concern about the Samaritans and Jews' relationship issues by informing her that if she knew who He is and the importance of living water, then she would gladly give Him the water (v. 10). Because she does not know, she focuses on the fact that Jesus does not have anything to draw the water from the well or drink the water, so why is He there? Jesus doesn't address this issue because it is not relevant to why He is speaking with her. Keener states, "That the one who is greater than Jacob does not argue the point with her; it is peripheral to the issue he wishes to drive home" (1993, 273).

The Samaritan woman does not know that Jesus is far greater and superior to Jacob. She does not who Jesus is, so their conversation is based on what she has been taught and learned. Her use of the words "our father Jacob" would have been offensive to any other Jew since "the Jewish people were children of Israel and the teaching that the Samaritans at best were half-breeds" (273). Jesus is not taken

back or offended by her questions. His purpose for interacting with her was beyond the history of the well or her family history; Jesus wanted her to experience a revelation about her own identity and self-worth with such depth and impact, that those around her would come to learn, see, and accept Him for themselves.

John 4:13–15
¹³ *Jesus answered and said unto her, Whosoever drinketh of this water shall thirst again:*

¹⁴ *But whosoever drinketh of the water that I shall give him shall never thirst; but the water that I shall give him shall be in him a well of water springing up into everlasting life.*

¹⁵ *The woman saith unto him, Sir, give me this water, that I thirst not, neither come hither to draw.*

Although the woman requested physical water, she does not realize that Jesus is inviting her to accept spiritual water that never runs dry (MacArthur, 1550). The Samaritan woman has focused her attention on the water in the well. Like many of us, she only thinks about what she can see or confirm to be true. The well goes deep and has water, but the living water that Jesus offers is deeper and life-giving. Many of the characters in John's Gospel take the words and responses of Jesus literally (Keener, 273) or did not understand how He can see and provide beyond a surface response, such as the disciples who disbelieve that Jesus could feed five thousand people with a little boy's lunch and have leftovers (John 6:1–15).

The idea of living water is derived from an Old Testament motif that describes God. In Jeremiah 2:13, God describes Himself in the midst of disobedient Jews as the "fountain of Living water" (1550). Other prophetic writings follow this metaphor when they look forward to "living waters will flow out of Jerusalem" (Zechariah 14:8). The point is that "living waters" are equated with the infinite, eternal life embodied in Jesus Christ. The woman needs the life-giving water that can only be accessed through Jesus (1550).

The Samaritan woman thinks that the living water that Jesus has offered her will make life better for her because she will have less work. She did not want to go to the well every day, as it was an arduous and heavy task. Why not hope someone could offer her a better way of life? However, Jesus is not removing her life circumstances, but offering a way for her to make her own changes from the inside to the outside.

John 4:16–19
16 *Jesus saith unto her, Go, call thy husband, and come hither.*

17 *The woman answered and said, I have no husband. Jesus said unto her, Thou hast well said, I have no husband:*

18 *For thou hast had five husbands; and he*

whom thou now hast is not thy husband: in that saidst thou truly.

19 *The woman saith unto him, Sir, I perceive that thou art a prophet.*

The Samaritan woman's inability to understand spiritual matters causes Jesus to abruptly turn the conversation to her physical situation. The fact that the woman has had five husbands is an indication of the social upheaval in her life. Her life lacked stability, and her spiritual life was deficient. Some scholars suggest she is having an intimate relationship with a man that she is not married to and perhaps cohabitating with him (1550).

Jesus plainly described to a woman He did not know her physical condition, and she realizes that He has spiritual insights that call for her acknowledgement (1550). Jesus keeps moving the conversation toward her understanding and accepting who He is, her inward change, and her outward expression of that change.

John 4:20–24
20 *Our fathers worshipped in this mountain; and ye say, that in Jerusalem is the place where men ought to worship.*

21 *Jesus saith unto her, Woman, believe me, the hour cometh, when ye shall neither in this mountain, nor yet at Jerusalem, worship the Father.*

22 *Ye worship ye know not what: we know what we worship: for salvation is of the Jews.*

23 But the hour cometh, and now is, when the true worshippers shall worship the Father in spirit and in truth: for the Father seeketh such to worship him.

24 God is a Spirit: and they that worship him must worship him in spirit and in truth.

Jews and Samaritans worshiped God, but the Samaritans worshiped God incompletely. Samaritans worshiped recognizing the Pentateuch's laws but chose Shechem as the place of worship because it was the place where Abraham built an altar (1550). On the other hand, the Jews chose Jerusalem to worship God by using the entire Hebrew Bible. There is no reason to debate the location of worship; true worship is experienced regardless of location. However, Jesus stresses that the time would come that where people worship will become immaterial and irrelevant.

The hour is an indication of Jesus' Passion, that He must die and rise from the dead. True worshipers will be identified not by geography or ritual, but the genuineness of their worship of Jesus. True worshipers express their worship through their heart (MacArthur, 2006). The statement "God is a Spirit" reflects who God is. God is invisible; His nature is spiritual and cannot be seen. The spiritual realm of life is much greater than the physical realm. They that worship Jesus do so as a mandate; it is not optional but a true representation of Him.

PRACTICAL APPLICATION

PERSONAL APPLICATION

1. For the next seven days, text a friend about your passion for worship, and invite them to worship with you. Discuss with your friends what you did and why.

2. Why is worship important to you? Keep a journal or diary that you write to describe the worship experience after Sunday or another day of the week. Read and reflect on your comments.

COMMUNITY APPLICATION

1. Attend a worship celebration different from your own tradition. For example, if you are United Methodist, attend an Apostolic church service, or if you are Baptist, go to a Catholic church. Share with others your thoughts with the various groups as to how each can work together.

2. Create a video or PowerPoint that you can share with others in your church or Sunday School about the various churches you visited. Invite the churches you visited to meet and see how they can work together and plan a food drive or help young children.

MEDITATION

Worship allows us to say thank You to God for divine protection. Godly worship is sincere, private as well as public, and at the same time, an indispensable requirement in serving Jesus. Regardless of our past problems, our current predicament, and the challenges yet to be faced, Jesus continues to show us preferential treatment. A Samaritan woman was ostracized and marginalized, but Jesus meets her at the point of her greatest need. She becomes our superhero because of her ability to stand in spite of trouble. She is a superhero because "greater is he that is in [her] than he that is in the world" (1 John 4:4). Others have given up on her, but Jesus stands up for her. Regardless of gender, social standing, or financial circumstances, worship is mandated for serving a God who always meets us in our greatest need. Worship Him!

PRAYER

O God, the Supreme Ruler of our lives! Our worship flourishes out our need to express supreme devotion to You. Lord God, words are insufficient to express ourselves to You. Authentic worship as an act of devotion deepens our commitment, feeds our spirit and sharpens our serving capabilities. You mandate forgiveness as part of Your divine makeup. You gave us Jesus, our Hero, our Priest, and our King of Kings. Ride on, King Jesus; no man can hinder my worship. God of light and love, You alone have seen me through when I wanted to give up and give in. In the darkest moments of life, with friends far and few between, You became my friend. At an old well, You met a battered woman, and You fed her spirit to live. We too come to the well alone looking to drink, seeking happiness and searching for joy, and there we met You face to face.

Thank You for looking past our weaknesses and faults, thank You for seeing the good in us when others can only see the bad, thank You for encouraging us to move forward rather than backward and accentuate the positive rather than negative. In Jesus' name, Amen.

BIBLIOGRAPHY

Achtemeier, Paul J. *Harper's Bible Dictionary*. 1st ed. San Francisco: Harper & Row, 1985. 1143.

Carson, D. A. *New Bible Commentary: 21st Century Edition*. 4th ed. Leicester, England; Downers Grove, Illinois: InterVarsity Press, 1994. John 4:4.

Dakes, Finis Jennings. *Dake Annotated Reference Bible*. Lawrenceville, Georgia: Dake Publishing, 1991. 96.

Elwell, Walter A. and Beitzel, Barry J. *Baker Encyclopedia of the Bible*. Grand Rapids, Michigan: Baker Book House, 1988. 2164.

Keener, Craig. *The IVP Bible Background Commentary – New Testament*. Downers Grove, Illinois: InterVarsity Press, 1993. 272-273.

Life Application Study Bible – NIV. Wheaton, Illinois and Grand Rapids, Michigan: Zondervan, 1993. 1745-1746.

MacArthur, John. *The MacArthur Study Bible*. Nashville, Tennessee: Thomas Nelson. 2006. 1550.

CHAPTER 7

SHARE THE GOOD NEWS

SCRIPTURE LESSON
Mark 5:1–19

....

BACKGROUND SCRIPTURES
Matthew 8:28–34; Mark 1:23; Luke 8:26–39; Acts 16:17; Hebrews 7:1

QUESTION
Word of mouth is the most effective promotional vehicle in marketing. With the advent of customer reviews, referral sites like Angie's List, and other social media platforms, people love to share when they have discovered something that worked for them. What recent discovery have you shared with your circle of friends and family?

HELP IS NEEDED!
Stanley and Kimberly were in a real bind. They were excited about their new baby girl, but with their little addition came much more responsibility—most notably, the need for quality child care. Stan and Kim were both professionals who made an above-average living, but they could not afford for either of them to lose their income for an extended period. Kim's maternity leave was up in about a month and they needed to figure out how to ensure that their precious Morgan would be in good hands. Kim's mom moved in for six months, but was not looking to relocate because she enjoyed her independence. One day Kim had lunch with some co-workers who were experienced moms of school-age kids. They were a great resource for Kim in helping her navigate through finding the best child care. The Lord truly blessed Kim to be led to a Christian nanny who came with credible references and impeccable experience in early childhood development, and they were able to conduct an extensive background check. Once little Morgan was six months old, Stan and Kim felt relieved to have her cared for at home by a reputable nanny. The Lord used her co-workers to save the day!

DISCUSSION

What was the importance of a good reputation in this story and in your life as a Christian? How did good witnesses work to solve Stanley and Kimberly's problem?

TRANSITION

In this lesson, Jesus is met with a man with a problem that only He can solve. The legion of demons living in this man's spirit knew who Jesus was and that their days were numbered, because His reputation as the Son of the Living God preceded Him.

SCRIPTURE VOCABULARY

Gadarene (also called Gerasene or Girgesenes)—A region located along the eastern shore of the Sea of Galilee, with a collection of villages and cities called Decapolis. The grouping of cities and villages bordered Palestine, Syria, and Jordan. The actual village where Jesus met the demoniac (possessed man) is believed to be on the outskirts of Gerasa, but in the Scriptures, the broader region was identified for recognition.

Legion—A Roman army unit of about 6,000 foot soldiers or mounted horsemen used in the Gospels to denote a great multitude.

SCRIPTURE REFERENCE

Mark 5:1–19

1 And they came over unto the other side of the sea, into the country of the Gadarenes.

2 And when he was come out of the ship, immediately there met him out of the tombs a man with an unclean spirit,

3 Who had his dwelling among the tombs; and no man could bind him, no, not with chains:

4 Because that he had been often bound with fetters and chains, and the chains had been plucked asunder by him, and the fetters broken in pieces: neither could any man tame him.

5 And always, night and day, he was in the mountains, and in the tombs, crying, and cutting himself with stones.

6 But when he saw Jesus afar off, he ran and worshipped him,

7 And cried with a loud voice, and said, What have I to do with thee, Jesus, thou Son of the most high God? I adjure thee by God, that thou torment me not.

8 For he said unto him, Come out of the man, thou unclean spirit.

9 And he asked him, What is thy name? And he answered, saying, My name is Legion: for we are many.

10 And he besought him much that he would not send them away out of the country.

11 Now there was there nigh unto the mountains a great herd of swine feeding.

12 And all the devils besought him, saying, Send us into the swine, that we may enter into them.

13 And forthwith Jesus gave them leave. And the unclean spirits went out, and entered into the swine: and the herd ran violently down a steep place into the sea, (they were about two thousand;) and were choked in the sea.

14 And they that fed the swine fled, and told it in the city, and in the country. And they went out to see what it was that was done.

15 And they come to Jesus, and see him that was possessed with the devil, and had the legion, sitting, and clothed, and in his right mind: and they were afraid.

16 And they that saw it told them how it befell to him that was possessed with the devil, and also concerning the swine.

17 And they began to pray him to depart out of their coasts.

18 And when he was come into the ship, he that had been possessed with the devil prayed him that he might be with him.

19 Howbeit Jesus suffered him not, but saith unto him, Go home to thy friends, and tell them how great things the Lord hath done for thee, and hath had compassion on thee.

MEMORY VERSE

But watch thou in all things, endure afflictions, do the work of an evangelist, make full proof of thy ministry (2 Timothy 4:5).

HOW DOES THE MEMORY VERSE APPLY TO YOUR SPIRITUAL LIFE?

_____

_____

_____

_____

_____

_____

LESSON FOCUS

When you have a vibrant relationship with the Lord or an experience that fuels your faith, it should compel you to share your story. There is always an occasion to give glory to God by telling others what He has done for you. Believers display supernatural ability when they are unashamed to bear witness of the goodness of the Lord.

BIBLE BACKGROUND

In the previous verses, Jesus showed His supernatural power over a mighty storm (Mark 4:35–41). After a full day of teaching multiple parables, Jesus gathered His team to travel to their next destination. While the others were up top, He retired to the stern and fell asleep. The storm grew more and more turbulent and the disciples were frightened to the point that they feared for their lives. Peter ran to where Jesus was sleeping and woke Him up to ask, "Rabbi, don't you care that we perishing?" (v. 38). Jesus woke up and rebuked the wind, saying, "Peace! Be still!" And immediately the wind stopped and all was calm (v. 39). Those who witnessed this miracle were in awe of what had occurred and received another convincing proof of Jesus' deity.

A miracle is defined by the dictionary as "an effect or extraordinary event in the physical world that surpasses all known human or natural powers and is ascribed to a supernatural cause." Jesus, in His earthly ministry, exerted great power and authority to accomplish what no human could do. As Jesus encounters the demoniac, we will see Him simply using His words to take dominion over what others could not subdue.

SCRIPTURE EXPLORATION
Mark 5:1–19

Jesus and the disciples had traveled the rough waters of the sea and were now headed into the country of Gadarenes. Although the seas had been very rough, the next encounter would be quite harrowing as well. Jesus meets a man who was possessed by demons and lived alone

in the cemetery. People were afraid of him, and he could not stay in town and live with family or friends. He was too dangerous and too strong, so the cemetery, the dead people, became his place of residence.

Mark 5:1–5
¹ *And they came over unto the other side of the sea, into the country of the Gadarenes.*

² *And when he was come out of the ship, immediately there met him out of the tombs a man with an unclean spirit,*

³ *Who had his dwelling among the tombs; and no man could bind him, no, not with chains:*

⁴ *Because that he had been often bound with fetters and chains, and the chains had been plucked asunder by him, and the fetters broken in pieces: neither could any man tame him.*

⁵ *And always, night and day, he was in the mountains, and in the tombs, crying, and cutting himself with stones.*

Jesus and His disciples reached shore after a tumultuous journey, only to be met by a man who was possessed and tormented by demons. In Matthew's account of the story, there are two men. This man lived alone in the cemetery and displayed violent behavior toward himself and others. There were numerous attempts to restrain him with shackles, but the unnamed man had evil spirits living in him that displayed abnormal strength and he could not be restrained. No one person was strong enough to contain him; day and night he could be found screaming, crying, and cutting himself with stones because of the torment. The devil truly made his life miserable, and he was a man with no hope of entering society. This man and others who knew of him were accustomed to his condition, and he was left in isolation to battle his demons alone.

Mark 5:6–9

6 *But when he saw Jesus afar off, he ran and worshipped him,*

7 *And cried with a loud voice, and said, What have I to do with thee, Jesus, thou Son of the most high God? I adjure thee by God, that thou torment me not.*

8 *For he said unto him, Come out of the man, thou unclean spirit.*

9 *And he asked him, What is thy name? And he answered, saying, My name is Legion: for we are many.*

Upon Jesus' arrival, the demons immediately recognized Him because of the power His very presence exuded. The devil fears the presence of God because he knows he cannot overtake Him. As believers, we have power in the name of Jesus because we do not come in our own authority but on His. Jesus as the Son of the Living God, God in the flesh, did not have to do or say much for the devil to know his fate. At Jesus' very presence, the demons shrieked and bowed in worship

to the true and living God; they begged Jesus not to do to them what they were doing to this man. Now the demons were on high alert that it was time for them to go, as Jesus had already commanded them to come out of this man.

Jesus in taking action did not deal directly with the man, but the demonic spirits who were inflicting the torment, when He commanded them to identify themselves: "What is thy name?" Their response (Legion) indicated the multitude of spirits inhabiting the man. With such a great number of spirits wreaking havoc on this man's life, it is no wonder why he sought to hurt himself and others to escape the affliction and torment.

Mark 5:10–14

10 *And he besought him much that he would not send them away out of the country.*

11 *Now there was there nigh unto the mountains a great herd of swine feeding.*

12 *And all the devils besought him, saying, Send us into the swine, that we may enter into them.* 13 *And forthwith Jesus gave them leave. And the unclean spirits went out, and entered into the swine: and the herd ran violently down a steep place into the sea, (they were about two thousand; and were choked in the sea.*

14 *And they that fed the swine fled, and told it in the city, and in the country. And they went out to see what it was that was done.*

The demonic spirits at work through this man begged Jesus not to send them away to their eternal punishment of outer darkness, "into the Abyss" (Luke 8:31). They wanted to continue to cause more pain and torment by seeking another host to live. The demons asked Jesus to send them into the swine, considered an unclean animal. Jesus cast the demons out of the man and sent them to the swine, which upon receipt of the demons, immediately went into a panic, lost control of itself, and drowned.

Mark 5:15–17

15 *And they come to Jesus, and see him that was possessed with the devil, and had the legion, sitting, and clothed, and in his right mind: and they were afraid.*

16 *And they that saw it told them how it befell to him that was possessed with the devil, and also concerning the swine.*

17 *And they began to pray him to depart out of their coasts.*

The residents, believed to be herdsmen and probably the owners of the drowned pigs, witnessed Jesus casting out the demons and ran off to the surrounding communities to spread the word about what happened. These people were witnesses of this great display of power as the former demoniac was now in his right mind. Jesus accomplished what none of them could by His very presence and powerful words. However, rather than being grateful for seeing their neighbor restored to sanity, the residents were upset and frightened by the occurrence. They could be afraid because of the power displayed or the destruction of their pigs. As the people gathered, they begged Jesus to leave their community.

Mark 5:18–19

18 *And when he was come into the ship, he that had been possessed with the devil prayed him that he might be with him.*

19 *Howbeit Jesus suffered him not, but saith unto him, Go home to thy friends, and tell them how great things the Lord hath done for thee, and hath had compassion on thee.*

Overwhelmed with joy, the man, now free from possession, wanted to leave his place of affliction and start a new life with Jesus. He has been given a new life and the opportunity to re-enter society. Jesus, rather than allowing this man to leave with Him, tells him to stay behind, go back to his family, and tell others what the Lord has done for him. Jesus leaves this man, who could now communicate his experience with God and tell others how God has had compassion on him. Jesus was not widely known in the region east of the Sea of Galilee, but this man would serve as the catalyst for the Gospel in this region. Scholars estimate that the region of Gerasenes would go on to be home to at least 13 churches.

PRACTICAL APPLICATION

PERSONAL APPLICATION

1. What is the power of our witness in a culture that seems fascinated with the supernatural? How can you become an instrument of God to display His power on earth today?

2. Write a customer review of God's power at work in our lives so that others will be motivated to try it themselves and glorify our Father in heaven.

COMMUNITY APPLICATION

1. When it comes to injustices plaguing our communities, the church is often seen as powerless, but that is not our history—Jesus by His very presence was able to send demons on the run. We have the power of the Word of God to live in His authority and do the same, but how can we do it? What areas in your community need to know the presence and power of Jesus?

2. How can we begin today to put our faith into action and make a difference?

MEDITATION

The hope of Christ's glory gives us the power to be a witness of God's goodness and mercy. We were not saved to sit but be sent to reach others so that they too may be set free. People wait on us to release God's power in their lives by speaking hope into their situation and giving them a new vision of the life they were meant to live, whole and complete in Jesus Christ. As the body of Christ, we remain in the earth to give people hope in God's love for them and the grace extended to them by faith in Jesus Christ. The free gift of salvation is available to all who will receive, but we have to be available and have the courage to tell the story.

PRAYER

Father in heaven, thank You for the authority and power of the name of Your Son Jesus to set the captives free. Lord, You came that we might have life more abundantly. Enable us by Your Holy Spirit to serve as a powerful and credible witness of Your work in our lives. Help us to spread the Word and be unashamed to tell what You delivered us from. Thank You for setting us on the path of righteousness to enjoy relationship with You. Thank You for the blessing of You. In the name of Jesus, amen.

BIBLIOGRAPHY

Halley, Henry H. *Halley's Bible Handbook, Deluxe Edition*. Grand Rapids, Michigan: Zondervan, 2007. 572-574.

Peloubet, F.N. & M.A. *Smith's Bible Dictionary*. Peabody, MA: Hendrickson Publishers, 1999. 201-202.

dictionary.reference.com/browse/miracle. Accessed July 28, 2014.

CHAPTER 8

PRAISING GOD WITH A NEW STEP

SCRIPTURE LESSON
Acts 3:1–10

BACKGROUND SCRIPTURES
Psalm 56:17; Acts 2:42–47, 3:11–26, 4:10, 16, 20, 14:8

QUESTION
When something exciting and extraordinary happens in your life that makes you feel good, how do you respond? Give an example.

HENRY'S DILEMMA

Henry's job was offering a special dinner with Broadway tickets, and Henry was excited to go. He had saved enough money to buy two tickets, put a down payment on his tux, and keep just enough in case he and his girlfriend decided to stop by for coffee and dessert after the play. Henry was ready to go, but then something happened to change everything. Someone had gone through the neighborhood and slashed the tires on cars parked on the street, including Henry's. Unfortunately, Henry did not have extra money to replace his tires. He would have to use his money for tickets and tux rental, and borrow $100 from his uncle to buy the tires. Even after the tires were purchased, he would not have any money left for any extra spending, and he would have to pay his uncle back.

Henry decided to take a deep breath and deal with the problem. What do you think Henry should do?

DISCUSSION

Sometimes we depend on others because our circumstances keep us from being fully able to completely care for ourselves. How does this make you feel and what are some reactions that you've had when you realized that you needed help?

TRANSITION

The characters of this Scripture include two men of God seeking to pray together in the temple. As they enter, they encounter a lame man laying by the gate called Beautiful. He became a beggar with his neighbors' help because they carried him to his special spot by the gate. This story outlines some of the necessary steps that God often uses to transform us from helpless beggars to joy-filled worshipers. Often we ask without seeking, see without looking, and attempt to fix without finding. Today's lesson will show us how God can use our most humbling circumstances to bring us the most fulfilling joy of our lifetime, if we refuse to allow ourselves to become beggars.

SCRIPTURE VOCABULARY

Alms—Giving charity donations that include money, food, clothes, or other items.

Beautiful (temple gate)—This gate was known for its exquisite beauty and design. It was made of Corinthian bronze and was located probably by the entrance to Courts of the Women.

SCRIPTURE REFERENCE

Acts 3:1–10

1 Now Peter and John went up together into the temple at the hour of prayer, being the ninth hour.

2 And a certain man lame from his mother's womb was carried, whom they laid daily at the gate of the temple which is called Beautiful, to ask alms of them that entered into the temple;

3 Who seeing Peter and John about to go into the temple asked an alms.

4 And Peter, fastening his eyes upon him with John, said, "Look on us."

5 And he gave heed unto them, expecting to receive something of them.

6 Then Peter said, Silver and gold have I none; but such as I have give I thee: In the name of Jesus Christ of Nazareth rise up and walk.

7 And he took him by the right hand, and lifted him up: and immediately his feet and ankle bones received strength.

8 And he leaping up stood, and walked, and entered with them into the temple, walking, and leaping, and praising God.

9 And all the people saw him walking and praising God:

10 And they knew that it was he which sat for alms at the Beautiful gate of the temple: and they were filled with wonder and amazement at that which had happened unto him.

MEMORY VERSE

I will praise thee for ever, because thou hast done it: and I will wait on thy name; for it is good before thy saints (Psalm 52:9).

HOW DOES THE MEMORY VERSE APPLY TO YOUR SPIRITUAL LIFE?

_____

_____

_____

_____

_____

_____

_____

LESSON FOCUS

Peter and John's healing of the crippled man is the prelude for Peter's preaching and teaching about Christ to those who had witnessed or wondered how the man had been healed.

BIBLE BACKGROUND

The book of Acts records certain phases of progress of Christianity for some thirty years after Jesus' death and resurrection. Today's lesson is taken from the first division of the Acts, about the formation and development of the church of Jerusalem. It is apparent that the books of Luke and Acts share the same author (Metzger, 1993, 7). The latest event recorded in Acts was Paul's spending two years under house arrest in Rome. This event occurs around 60 CE and most of the book deals with the twenty years preceding that date (Metzger 8). The one recipient of Acts is explicitly named—Theophilus. We know virtually nothing about him, but he could be regarded as a representative of the intelligent middle-class public of Rome, to which Luke wished to present a reliable account of the rise and progress of Christianity. Rome is the most likely place for the first publication of the work. Not only is Rome its goal, but with Paul's arrival there, Rome implicitly replaces Jerusalem as the center from which the faith is spread (Metzger 8).

Today's lesson uses the symbolism of a beggar's methods to show us the joy available when we trust what God has already equipped us with (Matthew 6:8). We must note that no one in this story had any money; Peter and John had a spiritual gift and the lame man had a condition. God uses their encounter to bring about "wonder and amazement" among those who were witnesses. When was the last time you allowed God to use your difficult circumstances to bring about "wonder and amazement" to those watching your public suffering? When was the last time that you "walked, leaped and praised God publicly" for the things that God's Spirit accomplished in your life?

SCRIPTURE EXPLORATION

We become like beggars when we ask God and others for the wrong things. We often make the mistake of evaluating our needs based upon our past failures and doubts instead of the many victories God has wrought in our lives. We commonly refuse to ask God for what we really need because it is too "big" rather than trusting that all earthly accomplishments are a small thing in God's sight (Genesis 1:1).

This text gives a great example of one asking of the men of God but not "seeking" the things of God. It further shows an example of one who "sees" the men of God but must be instructed to look. The lame man's friends had resolved that his best opportunity for blessing was to lay at the gate and rely on the temple goers' generosity; however, this only demonstrates our attempts to fix our problems without finding God's solution.

Acts 3:1
1 *Now Peter and John went up together into the temple at the hour of prayer, being the ninth hour.*

Peter and John walked together to the temple to pray during the ninth hour (3 p.m.). The temple was located on Mount Moriah in Jerusalem and was built by exiles returning from Babylonia. Peter and John are going to pray, and will also participate in a miracle of healing. Both men had experienced much as disciples of Jesus; they were both selected to be His disciples and were part of His inner circle, or top three men (Peter, James, and John). Peter was there when John and James asked who would sit at the "right hand of God," and John was probably there when Peter denied Jesus, but neither of those diminished the relationship from growing (John 18:6). Peter and John

ran to the sepulcher to see if Jesus was there after His crucifixion (John 20:6), and each experienced the pain of not always being at his best in Christ. Peter and John were there for each other during their difficult, rewarding, and challenging faith walk, and shared their faith and willingness to follow Christ and live a life as doers of the Word of God.

Peter and John point us to the great truth that when we pray together, great things are bound to happen. Men and women of faith praying together in the body of Christ is powerful; "Iron sharpeneth iron; so a man sharpeneth the countenance of his friend" (Proverbs 27:17). This focuses intentionally on the disciples' prayerful method for personal and spiritual empowerment through ministry. Jesus' disciples only made one request of Him: "Lord, teach us to pray, as John also taught his disciples" (from Luke 11:1).

These two disciples had not forgotten how to pray or how to "seek" God. Instead, they wondered, what was Jesus asking for during this time of prayer? Even Jesus had to pray. We ought to pray daily together. It is no coincidence that as Peter, John, and Jesus sought prayer time, a need for spiritual empowerment arose among the people around them.

Acts 3:2
2 *And a certain man lame from his mother's womb was carried, whom they laid daily at the gate of the temple which is called Beautiful, to ask alms of them that entered into the temple;*

As Peter and John entered the temple, a lame man was begging for alms. This man could not walk, and from birth had depended on others to meet many of his everyday needs. Begging was a common experience during this time. People who could not work would beg to receive alms. Caring for those in need was expected and required by God. The Jewish community expected others to provide for the needs of those who were in need or had to beg. Jesus' emphasizes caring and compassion in our own communities and beyond in the story of the Good Samaritan (Luke 10:25–37).

The Beautiful Gate was a popular title for the Nicanor Gate given by an Alexandrian donor, and situated on the east side of the temple where the women entered (Court of the Women) and beggars would find a place to wait. The gate was known for its design, the Corinthian bronze (the most expensive material), and its size—larger than the other gates. Josephus, the Jewish historian, described this gate, which separated the inner court from the outer Court of the Gentiles on the east, as the gate that "greatly excelled those that were only covered over with silver and gold." This gate was about 75 feet high and its huge double doors would have been opened wide at this hour to accommodate the foot traffic. (This was also a place where beggars would gather and ask for alms as people entered the temple.)

Although the man patiently waited as he begged by the temple, God had another plan for his life. He probably did not think other options existed for his healing or living a different life. The beggar was fixing his problem the best way he or anyone else knew how—begging.

We often attempt to fix our problems without finding God's real solution. If we tarry with God's complete solution, we will often find in the many miracle stories that His answer only uses the physical circumstance, but the ultimate answer is a spiritual breakthrough. God can manipulate all physical circumstances to His greater glory. We shouldn't be discouraged or impressed by physical circumstances; we will find once again here that we as believers shouldn't accept difficult circumstances because they have a way of changing suddenly (Psalm 37:36).

Our physical condition is not always our calling to contentment or acceptance; it could be a beseeching or imploring by God to push to do better. As people of faith. when the storms of our lives are bellowing and raging all around us, we ought to at least seek the solution of God amid our circumstance.

We are called to resist the temptation to assimilate for the sake of survival. Howard Thurman writes in *Jesus and the Disinherited*: "It is a profound capitulation to the powerful, because it means the yielding of oneself to that which, deep within, one recognizes as being unworthy, it makes for a strategic loss of self-respect." Assimilation means, in simplistic terms, acceptance. Can we afford to accept our infirmities and their existential baggage as God's destined plight for our lives? Can we afford to encourage anyone else to accept their plight in life as we claim to seek God in prayer?

Acts 3:3–6
³ *Who seeing Peter and John about to go into the temple asked an alms.*

⁴ *And Peter, fastening his eyes upon him with John, said, Look on us.*

⁵ *And he gave heed unto them, expecting to receive something of them.*

⁶ *Then Peter said, Silver and gold have I none; but such as I have give I thee: In the name of Jesus Christ of Nazareth rise up and walk.*

The beggar sees Peter and John come into the temple, so he decided he should ask for alms. After all, what kind of hypocrite could pass a lame man on their way to the temple and refuse to give alms? It is clear that the lame man never saw what was coming next.

Peter "fastened his eyes upon him" and told him to "Look at us." Thurman wrote that "it is the sin of pride and arrogance that has tended to vitiate the missionary impulse and to make of it an instrument of self-righteousness on the one hand and racial superiority on the other." Thurman wants us to resist the temptation of missionary zeal where we actually disdain those whom we claim to serve. Issues of racism, sexism, and economic

exploitation are often ignored or overlooked as normal or "not that bad." A praying man ought to be able to look beyond a person's exterior and find their need. The beauty here is that Peter and John knew what they had to give, and it wasn't money.

Peter tells the man that "Silver and gold have I none; but such as I have give I thee: In the name of Jesus Christ of Nazareth rise up and walk." The begging man was healed. All he had to do was stand up and a new life of walking, jumping, working, and so much more opened up to him. His healing happened because Peter healed in the name of Jesus. Jesus' name had the power, and he was the willing vessel. What a blessing when we are open to Jesus' power operating in our lives for others and ourselves.

Our Scripture lesson reminds us to evaluate our motives when we go to God and His people for assistance. Are we asking for anything we can get, or do we seek what God has in store for those who truly love Him? Jesus emphasizes this to us in Matthew 6:33: "But seek ye first the kingdom of God, and his righteousness; and all these things shall be added."

Acts 3:7–10
⁷ *And he took him by the right hand, and lifted him up: and immediately his feet and ankle bones received strength.*

⁸ *And he leaping up stood, and walked, and entered with them into the temple, walking, and leaping, and praising God.*

⁹ And all the people saw him walking and praising God:

¹⁰ And they knew that it was he which sat for alms at the Beautiful gate of the temple: and they were filled with wonder and amazement at that which had happened unto him.

Peter touched him! The man who could not walk began walking and praising the Lord (3:9). People were amazed at the miracle they witnessed! Jesus' ministry was a touching ministry (Matthew 9.20); there is healing in the touch. Note the progression from helplessness to joy. Peter "took him by the right hand"… he touched him! He "lifted him up"! What a novel concept! Poverty is one of the biggest businesses in America. Exploitation is the rule of thumb. The church cannot afford to function merely as a business. Rev. Gardener Taylor reminds us that it is a living organism that cares for the needs of others and must provide channels that supports its responsibility to feed the hungry and clothe the naked (Matthew 25:35–36).

Could it be that the lame man's physical ailment was not his greatest problem? Could it be that God found a way to address his greatest issue—that he had allowed physical circumstances to steal his joy? How many people do we pass daily who have allowed life circumstances to steal their joy? Divorce, surgery, downsizing, sickness, politics, accidents, friends, scandal, shame, pride, failure, children, etc. have weighed on their psyche to the point that they no longer have joy. They have resolved to fix their own problems without finding Luke's salvific Jesus. They see the church but have no interest in the things of God. They are asking anyone who will listen, not unlike the beggar, about solutions, but they can't get any satisfaction. When was the last time you felt like begging, and it turned into a blessing that caused wonder and amazement about God Almighty?

PRACTICAL APPLICATION

PERSONAL APPLICATION

1. Develop a prayer blog or writer cards that you can give to others in need who need to communicate with God or know that God really does care about them and their situation.

2. Pray for the sick in hospitals, churches, street corners, senior homes, and in your family. Partner with a friend or family member and plan ways that you can encourage and assist people who are ill. Begin with your family or close friends.

COMMUNITY APPLICATION

1. Partner with other community groups that provide care for those who are in need of food, clothing, and shelter. See how your church is already involved or may want to expand their ministry in other areas.

2. Write or lobby your local government officials to make sure health care

facilities are available in poor communities. You can expand your community and find ways to look into and assist worldwide health needs.

MEDITATION

Reaching beyond our circumstances requires work, responsibility, and determination on our part. Dr. Benjamin E. Mays nudges us into reality through his statement of eloquence and reality:

It must be borne in mind that the tragedy of life doesn't lie in not reaching your goal. The tragedy lies in having no goal to reach. It isn't a calamity to die with dreams unfulfilled, but it is a calamity not to dream. It is not a disaster to be unable to capture your ideal, but it is a disaster to have no ideal to capture. It is not a disgrace not to reach the stars, but it is a disgrace to have no stars to reach for. Not failure, but low aim is sin.

PRAYER

Dear God, bless us to be a blessing to others. Help us to see and respond as needed to those who are sick, homeless, and without someone to care for them. Open our eyes to see the injustice and the pain of others. Care for us in our time of needs. Bless us so that we can be a blessing to others. In Jesus' name we pray, amen.

BIBLIOGRAPHY

Metzger, Bruce. *The Oxford Companion to the Bible*. New York: Oxford University Press. 1993. 8-10.

Mays, Benjamin. *Quotable Quotes of Benjamin E. Mays*. New York: Vantage Press, 1983. 3.

Thurman, Howard. *Jesus and the Disinherited*. Boston, Massachusetts, Abingdon Press, 1949. 12-13.

http://www.bibleversestudy.com/acts/acts3-gate-called-beautiful.htm. Accessed October 8, 2014.

www.matchdoctor.com. Accessed October 10, 2014.

NOTES

_____

_____

_____

_____

_____

_____

CHAPTER 9

PROTECTION: WHO'S GOT YOUR BACK?

SCRIPTURE LESSON
1 Samuel 19:1–7

BACKGROUND SCRIPTURES
1 Samuel 18–19; Ephesians 6:11–19

QUESTION
Do you consider protection important? Can you recall a time in your life when you felt unprotected and vulnerable? How did you feel at the time?

HOME SAFE AND SOUND?

The Smith family returned home early morning from their trip. They were surprised to find their door already open. Looking inside, they discovered their TV, computer, and other electronics were missing, as well as most of their jewelry and other valuables. The Smiths were shocked. They had felt safe in their house for years and had never been victims of a crime. They called the police, but since there had been no witnesses, the cops informed them that it was unlikely they would find their things again.

The Smiths were discouraged, and had a family meeting about what to do next.

They admitted they felt shaken by the experience, and no longer felt safe in their neighborhood. Since they could not afford to move yet, they decided instead to invest in a security system. Soon they had key codes to enter every time they wanted to enter or exit the house, and bars now covered the windows.

A few weeks later, Mr. Smith went out to run an errand while the rest of the family was at work or school. He came back to find police cars around his neighbor's house. She had heard a knock at the door, and when she went to answer, a man tried to force his way inside. Fortunately she had been able to call the police before anything happened.

That night, the Smiths all felt disturbed. They couldn't guard their home every minute of the day, but nothing they did seem to make them feel safe anymore. Was full protection possible?

DISCUSSION

Read about the whole armor of God in Ephesians 6:11–19. What part of the body does not have protection? Why do you think this is so and how can protection for it be obtained?

If you are thinking the back, you are certainly correct. A soldier should never turn his back to the enemy. However, if circumstances cause you to turn your back to the enemy, have no fear—God's got your back. That is why it needs no protection.

TRANSITION

This lesson from the Old Testament tells the story of Jonathan and David's friendship and how Jonathan did not allow his father's intense hatred of David to affect his friendship and loyalty. In fact, we will see that Jonathan had David's back. He defended his friend even at the peril of his own life. Do you have friends like that in your life? More fundamentally, are you that kind of friend?

Today Christians must be careful to maintain both their passion for God and their divine protection. It can be easy to get sucked up into denying any absolutes, moral responsibility, and divine existence. The notion that we must develop the God

within us is so very attractive, but it is a repetition of the first lie. How can we develop protection against such seductions and preserve our faith? Are these still relevant aspirations or vestiges from an outdated past?

We also live in an age when people become disappointed by their heroes. Many youths are adrift on a sea of meaninglessness, searching for meaning. How can we be to them what Jonathan was for David—a genuine friend who defended him and secured his protection? What can we learn from their example?

SCRIPTURE VOCABULARY

Delighted—Jonathan had high regards for David. He respected him and thought the utmost of him as a person and friend.

Heed—To be careful, keeping out of harm's way.

Commune—To converse or have conversation with or to talk over. Merriam-Webster says it is "to communicate with someone or something in a very personal or spiritual way."

Sin—In this biblical text, refers to wrong, harm, or hurt.

Salvation—Jonathan told his father that through David, God had "wrought a great salvation for all Israel." This means deliverance or rescue from the enemy.

SCRIPTURE REFERENCE

1 Samuel 19:1–7

¹ And Saul spake to Jonathan his son, and to all his servants, that they should kill David.

² But Jonathan Saul's son delighted much in David: and Jonathan told David, saying, Saul my father seeketh to kill thee: now therefore, I pray thee, take heed to thyself until the morning, and abide in a secret place, and hide thyself:

³ And I will go out and stand beside my father in the field where thou art, and I will commune with my father of thee; and what I see, that I will tell thee.

⁴ And Jonathan spake good of David unto Saul his father, and said unto him, let not the king sin against his servant, against David; because he hath not sinned against thee, and because his works have been to thee-ward very good:

⁵ For he did put his life in his hand, and slew the Philistine, and the LORD wrought a great salvation for all Israel: thou sawest it, and didst rejoice: wherefore then wilt thou sin against innocent blood, to slay David without a cause?

⁶ And Saul hearkened unto the voice of Jonathan: and Saul sware, As the LORD liveth, he shall not be slain.

⁷ And Jonathan called David, and Jonathan shewed him all those things. And Jonathan brought David to Saul, and he was in his presence, as in times past.

MEMORY VERSE

Deliver me, O LORD, from mine enemies: I flee unto thee to hide me (Psalm 143:9).

WHAT DOES THE MEMORY VERSE APPLY TO YOUR SPIRITUAL LIFE?

_____

_____

_____

_____

_____

_____

LESSON FOCUS

We live at a time when it is challenging to be Black or Latino on our country, and we need people who will protect and defend each other and our rights. Too many of us do not want to get involved or are content to let things be. Nazism succeeded in Europe because there were too few people who stood up to defend and protect. Many saw evil, but did not stand up against it because it didn't affect them. By the time they were affected, it was too late; no one was left to speak, defend, and protect.

Furthermore, we often look in the wrong places for role models. We pay homage

74

to athletes and celebrities and look over those who do more important work in the world and their community. Many celebrities do not know what to do with their newfound attention, saying they "don't want to be role models," and quickly prove unworthy of admiration. Who should we be looking to for guidance?

Real heroes are not such solely by virtue of their brawn, talent, good looks, or abilities. Instead, they are those who protect the vulnerable, give voice to the voiceless, and defend the marginalized. True heroes stand for God and for right, and endeavor to give attention to Him, not themselves.

BIBLE BACKGROUND

Our Scripture points to the time when Saul was king of a united Israel, about a thousand years or so before Christ. The Children of Israel were emerging from the times of the Judges. Contrary to God's wishes, they had rejected theocracy, gotten their first king, and now were learning the ways of a monarchy.

After David killed Goliath and had brought his head to the king, Saul wouldn't let him return home to his occupation as shepherd (1 Samuel 18:2). He saw potential and promise in David, so he took him to the palace to be an officer in his court, and a permanent attaché to the royal household. As court officer, David accompanied the king wherever the king went (18:5), and was given the task of overseeing the men of war (v. 5). He also served as resident musician and

helped calm the king's nervous condition and depression. Thus as bodyguard and "commander of [the] army" (Merrill 449), David was vital to the king's household and travel entourage. His wise behavior and good decorum won him the love and respect of all Israel and the protection of the Lord (vv. 14–16). Though the Lord was guiding David and had put him in the palace to learn the ways of royalty, Saul must be credited for recognizing potential and acting to ensure its development. God had given him a great opportunity to help David. Had he acted to mentor David and shared thoughts and ideas with him, he would have been remembered positively.

Unfortunately, while all this was transpiring, Saul increasingly began to grow suspicious of David. David's slaying Goliath did not go unnoticed; the women began singing, "Saul hath slain his thousands and David his ten thousands" (v. 7). These sentiments displeased Saul and caused him to begin to "eye David from that day and forward" (v. 9). Driven by depression and insanity, the very next day he attempted to kill David himself; when he failed, Saul became afraid of him (v. 15). However, he still wanted him dead, so he promised David his eldest daughter if he would fight the Philistines, hoping that David would die in the battle. His real motives became apparent when he gave her to someone else to marry.

Saul ultimately promised another daughter, Michal, in marriage to David hoping that "she may be a snare to him, and that the hand of the Philistines may be against him" (v. 21). Saul threw in a caveat, however; he asked no dowry from David, only a hundred Philistine foreskins as revenge against his enemies. His hope was that David would be killed in the process. David brought him not 100, but 200 foreskins. When Saul saw this and how his daughter loved David, he decided that God was with David. Saul feared him even more and became his enemy.

SCRIPTURE EXPLORATION

1 Samuel 19:1

[1] *And Saul spake to Jonathan his son, and to all his servants, that they should kill David.*

Given the place of prominence David had achieved in Saul's court, it means that when Saul gave orders to his son and all his servants to kill David, he was actually commissioning the murder and death of someone who was an officer in his court, a permanent attaché to his royal household, his army commander, and his son-in-law—an incredibly callous act. However, Jonathan acted with wisdom, integrity, and prudence. He was in a unique position to help his friend; his father Saul had taken him into his confidence. He wisely did not confront his father; instead he waited for the appropriate time and took time to warn David.

1 Samuel 19:2–3

[2] *But Jonathan Saul's son delighted much in David: and Jonathan told David, saying, Saul my father seeketh to kill thee:*

now therefore, I pray thee, take heed to thyself until the morning, and abide in a secret place, and hide thyself:

[3] *And I will go out and stand beside my father in the field where thou art, and I will commune with my father of thee; and what I see, that I will tell thee.*

Unlike his father, Jonathan became close to David from the first day they met. They became soulmates, kindred spirits, and fast friends. Spence-Jones observes "... a friend-ship was the result which ranks among the purest and the noblest examples of true manly affection. The word rendered knit literally means knotted, tied together firmly by indissoluble bonds" (Spence-Jones, 339). They entered into a pact of friendship in which they swore to be steadfast friends.

Imagine David—the country shepherd boy—in the king's palace! He needed a new wardrobe suited for a courtier. His new friend came to his rescue. Keil and Delitzsch suggest that "As a sign and pledge of his friendship, Jonathan gave David his clothes and his armour" (Keil 490). Freeman suggests that even his sword, bow, and belt were included. He also notes that it was a special mark of respect for a prince to give someone the garments he was wearing. Moreover, the gift of a belt is a symbol of the greatest confidence and friendliness, and was greatly cherished (Freeman 214).

Their strong bond made Jonathan fiercely loyal to David. It is not surprising that

Jonathan would have risked his own life and safety to tell David the truth: Saul hated and planned to kill him His was a difficult position—to choose between loyalty to his father or his friend. Because of their bond of friendship, he chose loyalty to David, who he thought did not deserve death. He warned David to take heed and find a safe place to hide. Jonathan even told David that he would speak directly to his father, promising to meet and converse with him and report back so David could be aware of his true standing with the king.

1 Samuel 19:4–5

4 *And Jonathan spake good of David unto Saul his father, and said unto him, Let not the king sin against his servant, against David; because he hath not sinned against thee, and because his works have been to thee-ward very good:*

5 *For he did put his life in his hand, and slew the Philistine, and the Lord wrought a great salvation for all Israel: thou sawest it, and didst rejoice: wherefore then wilt thou sin against innocent blood, to slay David without a cause?*

True to his word, Jonathan met with his father and began a discussion of his relationship with David. He spoke good words about David, then pled not to sin against David, since contrary to his beliefs, David had not sinned against him but was very loyal. He reminded Saul of how David had disregarded his own life to fight and kill Goliath. He recapped for him how the Lord had wrought a great

salvation for Israel through David, which he had seen and rejoiced about himself. Finally, Jonathan challenged the moral sensibilities of his father, suggesting that to kill David would be sin against innocent blood without cause. Jonathan certainly was trying to protect and defend his friend. He certainly had his best interests at heart; his example indeed can speak to youths today and give them a role model to emulate.

1 Samuel 19:6

6 *And Saul hearkened unto the voice of Jonathan: and Saul sware, As the LORD liveth, he shall not be slain.*

This verse confirms that Jonathan was successful in his advocacy, persuading his father to see that David was innocent. Saul responds positively to his son and swears with the Lord as his witness that he would not kill David. Jamieson, Fausset, and Brown state: "The strong remonstrances of Jonathan produced an effect on the impulsive mind of his father. As he was still susceptible of good and honest impressions, he bound himself by an oath to relinquish his hostile purpose; and thus, through the intervention of the noble-minded prince, a temporary reconciliation was effected, in consequence of which David was again employed in the public service" (Jaimeson, 1 Samuel 19:4).

At least for a time, Jonathan's words positively impacted him. Perhaps Saul meant it at the time, but eventually he did not keep his word. Today's society may have characterized him as bipolar or manic-depressive. He seemed unable to act consistently; one moment he was calm and collected, the next raging mad and aggressive. His condition clearly speaks to what happens when one goes their own way and is no longer under the leadership, guidance, and influence of the Holy Spirit. We all need to pray to ensure the Lord in our lives because "there but for the grace of God goes I."

1 Samuel 19:7

7 *And Jonathan called David, and Jonathan shewed him all those things. And Jonathan brought David to Saul, and he was in his presence, as in times past.*

Confident with his successful advocacy, Jonathan shared the outcome with David and took him home. He took David to Saul and the record says David "was in his presence as in times past," thanks to Jonathan, who defended and protected his friend and brother. He was well-meaning and did his part; one cannot expect any more than that.

PRACTICAL APPLICATION

PERSONAL APPLICATION

1. Send a tweet or write a Facebook message to a young person to encourage them in their pursuits and develop a supportive posture for them, using the story of Jonathan as an inspiration.

2. Pray at least once a week for the safety, health, and well-being of our young people. Keep a record or journal of your prayer time and any changes in the lives of young people you know. Share your prayer requests with another prayer warrior and partner together to pray at least once a month for young people.

COMMUNITY APPLICATION

1. Young men and women are an endangered species in today's society. What can you do to protect and ensure a future for them? To succeed, they need positive relationships in their live. What difference might your support and encouragement make them? Find a young person that you might develop a supportive bond with to help them do well in life and in their academic pursuits. All you may need to do is give a weekly reminder to do well in school or their work.

2. Give a short five-minute talk to a youth group or Sunday School class sharing the difference that a person who rescued or helped you made in your life.

MEDITATION

Find a quiet spot in your home or environment. Retreat there, and in quiet solitude, think back on people in your life that were supportive and protective of you. Thank God for them and commit to reciprocate for others what was done for you.

PRAYER

Dear God: Thank you for designing and creating this beautiful world, despite its many problems. Thank You for the example of Jonathan; help us to model his example. Thank You for _____ who were an example for me. Bless them. Help me realize that whether I know it or not, I am an example for someone. Help me to intentionally act to defend and protect at least one of Your needy children for whom You died and for whom it is so challenging to just live, today. I love You, Lord. Please come soon to end earth's woe and strife and take us to be with You forever. Thank You Father God. Amen.

BIBLIOGRAPHY

Freeman, James M. and Harold J. Chadwick. *The New Manners and Customs of the Bible*. North Brunswick, NJ: Bridge-Logos Publishers, 1998.

Jamieson, Robert, A.R. Fausset, and David Brown. *Commentary Critical and Explanatory on the Whole Bible*. Oak Harbor, WA: Logos Research Systems, Inc., 1997.

Keil, C. F. and F. Delitzsch. *Commentary on the Old Testament*. Peabody: Hendrickson Publishers, Inc., 1996.

Merrill, Eugene H. "1 Samuel," in *The Bible Knowledge Commentary: An Exposition of the Scriptures*, ed. J. F. Walvoord and R. B. Zuck, vol. 1. Wheaton, IL: Victor Books, 1985.

Omanson, Roger L. and John E. Ellington. *A Handbook on the First Book of Samuel*, UBS Handbook Series. New York: United Bible Societies, 2001.

Peterson, Eugene H. The Message. Bible Gateway. Accessed October 25, 2012.

Spence-Jones, H. D. M., ed., 1 Samuel, *The Pulpit Commentary*. New York: Funk & Wagnalls Company, 1909.

NOTES

_____

_____

_____

_____

_____

_____

_____

CHAPTER 10

WORK ETHIC: ADVANCING THE GOOD NEWS

SCRIPTURE LESSON

Acts 18:1–4, 18–26

BACKGROUND SCRIPTURES

Acts 13:1–4; Romans 16:3–4; 1 Corinthians 3:5–9, 16:19

QUESTION

What characteristics drew Paul to Aquila and Priscilla? Think about your working relationships on the job and in the church. What causes you to gravitate to certain people?

WEARING TWO HATS

Pastor Lincoln was celebrating his 7th pastoral anniversary and another church was invited to share in the celebration. Their pastor, J. McDaniels, was the guest preacher and their children's and gospel choir sang. After the worship celebration, both churches and guests greeted one another as refreshments and appetizers were served. During this fellowship time, one woman, Yvette, saw someone she had not seen in 12 years—Danielle. They used to belong to the same church and volunteered at the shelter for homeless women. Both Yvette and Danielle reminisced about some of the funny moments they shared.

Danielle and Yvette were then shocked to

see a special friend, Christopher Delmar. Danielle and Christopher had gone to high school together. After introducing Yvette to Christopher, they quickly all shared what they were doing with their lives. Christopher shared that he was now a minister and working as a manager of a construction company. He and his wife worked to support themselves and help with church expenses because the congregation was small and could not afford the cost of running the church and paying a pastor.

Christopher was grateful that he was a construction manager and that his wife was supportive of the church's needs. As a "tentmaker" pastor, he was able to provide for his family and serve the church.

Christopher told us that he is working with a team to review and plan the financial needs of the church, and how to grow the church spiritually, financially, and in their community.

Many pastors are motivated to serve as "tentmaker," or bi-vocational, pastors to advance the Gospel while working full-time secular jobs during the week. Their ministry includes pastoring, preaching, and providing a model of Christian work ethic.

DISCUSSION

Do you know any tentmaker pastors? How do they minister the Gospel to people who may never visit their churches?

TRANSITION

Tentmaker pastors wear two hats: working full time during the week and pastoring on the weekend as well as probably one night during the week. Are there any advantages of husband and wife partnering in ministry?

SCRIPTURE VOCABULARY

Antioch—A city in modern Turkey, near the northeast corner of the Mediterranean Sea. Disciples of Jesus were first called Christians at Antioch (Acts 11:26).

Apollos—A Jew from Alexandria who spoke boldly in the synagogue, taught by Priscilla and Aquila.

Aquila and Priscilla—A Christian couple, fellow workers with Paul, and teachers of the Gospel.

Corinth—A commercial and manufacturing city of Greece, about 40 miles west of Athens. The Apostle Paul founded a church in Corinth and wrote letters to them (1 and 2 Corinthians).

Ephesus—Capital of the Roman province of Asia. Many Jews were established at Ephesus; Paul preached there for over two years.

Tentmakers—Tentmakers, used in a contemporary setting, are Christians motivated to support themselves while doing ministry; bi-vocational ministers who work secular full-time jobs. A traditional tentmaker is someone who makes tent(s)—small to large coverings used mainly for outdoor events, but can include indoor activities as well. Tents can be used from various events that may range from camping to church revivals. The Apostle Paul, Priscilla, and Aquila made tents for a living.

SCRIPTURE REFERENCE

Acts 18:1–4

1 After these things Paul departed from Athens, and came to Corinth;

2 And found a certain Jew named Aquila, born in Pontus, lately come from Italy, with his wife Priscilla; (because that

Claudius had commanded all Jews to depart from Rome:) and came unto them.

3 And because he was of the same craft, he abode with them, and wrought: for by their occupation they were tentmakers.4 And he reasoned in the synagogue every sabbath, and persuaded the Jews and the Greeks.

Acts 18:18–26

18 And Paul after this tarried there yet a good while, and then took his leave of the brethren, and sailed thence into Syria, and with him Priscilla and Aquila; having shorn his head in Cenchrea: for he had a vow.

19 And he came to Ephesus, and left them there: but he himself entered into the synagogue, and reasoned with the Jews.

20 When they desired him to tarry longer time with them, he consented not;

21 But bade them farewell, saying, I must by all means keep this feast that cometh in Jerusalem: but I will return again unto you, if God will. And he sailed from Ephesus.

22 And when he had landed at Caesarea, and gone up, and saluted the church, he went down to Antioch.

23 And after he had spent some time there, he departed, and went over all the country of Galatia and Phrygia in order, strengthening all the disciples.

24 And a certain Jew named Apollos, born at Alexandria, an eloquent man, and mighty in the scriptures, came to Ephesus.

25 This man was instructed in the way of the Lord; and being fervent in the spirit, he spake and taught diligently the things of the Lord, knowing only the baptism of John.

26 And he began to speak boldly in the synagogue: whom when Aquila and Priscilla had heard, they took him unto them, and expounded unto him the way of God more perfectly.

MEMORY VERSE

For as the body without the spirit is dead, so faith without works is dead also (James 2:26).

HOW DOES THE MEMORY VERSE APPLY TO YOUR SPIRITUAL LIFE?

_____

_____

_____

_____

_____

_____

LESSON FOCUS

The main focus of this lesson is to show that God uses people's work ethics and their spiritual gifts to advance the spread of the Gospel.

BIBLE BACKGROUND

The book of Acts is referred to as "the Acts of the Apostles" and the second of a two-volume book (Luke-Acts) written by Luke and dedicated to a Roman official named Theophilus. Luke was a traveling companion of Paul during some of his missionary journeys (Colossians 4:14; Philemon 24; 2 Timothy 4:11). While there is no precise date for the writing of Acts, possible dates include A.D. 64 and, based on Acts 24:27, as late as A.D. 80–90.

Luke's purpose in writing is primarily proclamation of the Word of God and to show its roots and interactions with history, its universal character, and the power and activity of the Holy Spirit. Luke devotes substantial space to Paul's missionary journeys, demonstrating knowledge of disagreements among missionary teams, geography of the land, early expansion and spread of Christianity to Asia Minor, as well as Paul's reason for traveling: preaching to the Jews and Gentiles.

Chapter 18 covers some of Paul's second missionary journey and shows him as a tentmaker preacher. This chapter also includes the work of a husband and wife team, Priscilla and Aquila, who were tentmakers. Paul met them in Corinth and stayed with them. Aquila and Priscilla also helped to advance the Good News by teaching Apollos, a man they met in Ephesus who knew about spiritual things. He had a vigorous personality and had been a disciple of John the Baptist, but Apollos was limited in knowledge of God's Word. Not all religious people have been taught the way of God accurately, or they might have limited knowledge and understanding of His Word.

SCRIPTURE EXPLORATION

This section of chapter 18 involves the following incidents: 1) Paul meets Aquila and Priscilla in Corinth;2) Paul advances the Good News in Palestine-Syria; and 3) Aquila and Priscilla advance the Good News. The Gospel of Jesus Christ is shared through Paul, Aquila, Priscilla, and Apollos. Although Paul is a major part of advancing the Good News in the book of Acts, we find that he has taught and encouraged others to share God's Word. Paul encouraged those who were willing disciples to keep sharing and moving the kingdom of God forward. He reminds us that we must share the Good News and develop disciples who will advance the message of Christ, e.g., truth, salvation, love, justice, and forgiveness.

Learning the truth of God's Word is key to advancing the message of Christ. Aquila and Priscilla assisted Apollos to become stronger and grounded in Christ's message. Through their love, knowledge of the Word, and guidance, both Aquila and Priscilla educated

Apollos. It is still important today to have teachers that correctly teach and provide direction for those who want to learn more about Christ. Advancing the Good News that builds the kingdom of God also requires a commitment to learn, and a desire to witness to the Good News of Christ and live God's Word.

Acts 18:1–4

¹ *After these things Paul departed from Athens, and came to Corinth;*

² *And found a certain Jew named Aquila, born in Pontus, lately come from Italy, with his wife Priscilla; (because that Claudius had commanded all Jews to depart from Rome:) and came unto them.*

³ *And because he was of the same craft, he abode with them, and wrought: for by their occupation they were tentmakers.*

⁴ *And he reasoned in the synagogue every sabbath, and persuaded the Jews and the Greeks.*

After Paul left Athens, he came to Corinth, the greatest commercial city of Greece. Corinth was situated on a four-mile wide land and was a proud and wealthy seaport, with Cenchrea on the east and Lechaeum on the west. Although the city had been destroyed in 146 B.C. by the Roman consul, Julius Caesar rebuilt the city in 46 B.C., also constructing statues and fountains. Corinth was known for its statue of Aphrodite, goddess of love and fertility, that dominated the social and religious life; immorality

was popular among its citizens and travelers. Amid this social and religious climate, the Apostle Paul came to Corinth in A.D. 50 and stayed about a year and a half teaching the Word of God. There he met a Christian couple named Aquila and Priscilla, who became co-laborers in the tentmaking trade.

The Christian couple had been forced to leave Rome because of Emperor Claudius's edict against the Jews. They were tentmakers, a craft that Apostle Paul apparently learned as a Jewish boy, fashioning tent material from goat's hair or tanned goatskins. Paul worked as a tentmaker to support himself on his missionary journeys, while also preaching in the synagogue every Sabbath. According to an article in the Theology of Work Project, "Luke's orienting idea for Christian life is that of witness and, the entirety of one's life has potential to bear witness." Since Paul's occupation was the same as the Christian couple, he stayed with them and they worked together as tentmakers.

Acts 18:18–22

¹⁸ *And Paul after this tarried there yet a good while, and then took his leave of the brethren, and sailed thence into Syria, and with him Priscilla and Aquila; having shorn his head in Cenchrea: for he had a vow.*

¹⁹ *And he came to Ephesus, and left them there: but he himself entered into the synagogue, and reasoned with the Jews.*

20 When they desired him to tarry longer time with them, he consented not;

21 But bade them farewell, saying, I must by all means keep this feast that cometh in Jerusalem: but I will return again unto you, if God will. And he sailed from Ephesus.

22 And when he had landed at Caesarea, and gone up, and saluted the church, he went down to Antioch

Paul stayed in Corinth for a considerable length of time. In the spring of A.D. 52, Paul and his co-workers sailed to Antioch (the capital of Syria). Paul had cut his hair in Cenchrea (Acts 18:18, Numbers 6:16–21) and was anxious about going to Jerusalem to keep a feast and perform the rites of the Nazarite law. He left Priscilla and Aquila in Ephesus, went to Caesarea, and saluted the church at Jerusalem.

At the time of Christ and Paul, Caesarea, a busy seaport with a great commercial center and a mammoth harbor, was located by the sea about 32 miles north of Joppa and 60 miles north of Jerusalem. After spending some time there, Paul traveled all over Galatia and Phrygia advancing the Good News of God and strengthening all the disciples.

Acts 18:23–26
23 And after he had spent some time there, he departed, and went over all the country of Galatia and Phrygia in order, strengthening all the disciples.

24 And a certain Jew named Apollos, born at Alexandria, an eloquent man, and mighty in the scriptures, came to Ephesus.

25 This man was instructed in the way of the Lord; and being fervent in the spirit, he spake and taught diligently the things of the Lord, knowing only the baptism of John.

26 And he began to speak boldly in the synagogue: whom when Aquila and Priscilla had heard, they took him unto them, and expounded unto him the way of God more perfectly.

Ephesus, the fourth largest city of the Roman Empire and the capital of Asia, was a deeply religious ancient city; the chief devotion was to Artemis, a goddess of wildness and fertility. Paul labored in Ephesus for about three years and laid a foundation for the strongest Christian church during the first century. But as Christianity became more popular, worship of Artemis declined, prompting a riot against Paul.

Paul had left Aquila and Priscilla in Ephesus, and while there, they met a Jew named Apollos from Alexandria. He was an eloquent, bold, and diligent spokesman of the Scriptures. But when Apollos, who had only been instructed in the ways of John the Baptist, began to speak in the synagogue, Aquila and Priscilla recognized that he should be taught the way of Christ. So they took Apollos aside and taught him the Good News of God, thus advancing Christianity in Ephesus.

PRACTICAL APPLICATION

PERSONAL APPLICATION

1. Search the Internet to find information about the challenges, concerns, and cross-cultural work of other tentmaker pastors. Start a daily blog that will attract people looking for information about Christians who are tentmaker pastors.

2. Pray at least once a week for all pastors, particularly those who work additional jobs to support themselves, their families, and their church.

COMMUNITY APPLICATION

1. Apollos was an educated Jew born in Alexandria, who immigrated to Ephesus because the Jews were commanded to leave Rome. Collaborate with other churches and community organizations to set up a scholarship fund for a student who is an immigrant and a student who is a member of your church to continue in school for one year (check with local colleges and universities to see their needs and criteria), based on established criteria and guidelines. A church or community organization might host workshops that assist in the application process for scholarship funds to support an aspiring teacher who is also pastoring.

2. Partner with other churches to create a program that helps feed and clothe children and families who live in communities in economic need. Build relationships with churches that want to serve the community but may have limited resources.

MEDITATION

The word "tentmaker" can only be found in the Bible in Acts 18:3. Luke describes Paul's craft as the reason he stayed with Aquila and Priscilla. Luke also mentions in Acts 20:34 that Paul uses his hands as the means of ministering to his necessities, and in 1 Corinthians 4:12, Paul says, "he labors with his hands." We are grateful for Paul's witness of modeling a Christian work ethic. Our Heavenly Father who created us has given us hands for a purpose: to support and care for ourselves, but we can also use our hands to help others. Meditate on the many ways that God uses your hands.

PRAYER

Father God, thank You for creating us with our hands. You gave us hands to feed ourselves, to work at various trades and professions and to be used for ministry. Thank You for this part of our body governed by the power of our minds and suggestions we receive from others. Keep our minds stayed on You for guidance in how to be a blessing with our hands. In Jesus' name, we pray. Amen.

BIBLIOGRAPHY

Barker, Kenneth L. and Kohlenberger, John R., III. *The Expositor's Bible Commentary Abridged Edition, New Testament*. Grand Rapids, Michigan: Zondervan Corp, 1994. 482-483.

Felder, Cain Hope, General Editor. *The Original African Heritage Study Bible, King James Version*. Nashville, Tennessee: James C. Winston Publishing Company, 1994. 1604-1606.

Peloubet, F.N. and M.A. *Smith's Bible Dictionary, Revised and Edited*. Nashville, Tennessee: Thomas Nelson Publishers, 1986.

Wansbrough, Henry, General Editor. *The New Jerusalem Bible, Standard Edition*. New York, NY, Doubleday, 1999.

Wright, Ernest, Principal Adviser and Editorial Consultant. *Great People of the Bible and How They Lived*. Sydney, Australia: The Reader's Digest Association, Inc. 1974. 404-407.

Bible Explorer 3 Edition, King James Edition (Acts 18:1-4, 18-26), July 2005-2006: Accessed July 12, 2014.

www.theologyofwork.org. Theology of Work Project, Accessed July 19, 2014.

www.wordpress.com. Accessed July 19, 2014.

www.worldwidetentmakers.com. What is a tent-maker? Accessed July 14, 2014.

www.pcusa.org/news/2012. Trusting God to Provide. Accessed July 14, 2014.

NOTES

NOTES